Hessdalen lights!

- what's happening in the Norwegian mountains?

Nils M. Ofstad

--

Thank's to Jadie Rachel Sten

for great help with the translation

Copyright © 2019 Nils M. Ofstad

All rights reserved.

ISBN: 978-0-359-60945-1

CONTENTS

1	Background	1
2	Trip to Sweden and a pit stop	11
3	A glimpse of the phenomenon	17
4	"15 meters!"	22
5	Easter in Hessdalen	31
6	"You won't see anything, anyway!"	38
7	The more sources the more reliable data	45
8	Light juni nights	51
9	Hide and seek	60
10	"You should have been with me!"	71
11	More satellites	86
12	Getting close is easier said than done	96
13	Fooled	106
14	"Knud"	112
15	Flash	118
16	Solution in six years? Sceptical!	128

1 BACKGROUND

The acronym *UFO* stands for *unidentified flying objects*, but in practice - in media, and elsewhere - the term has long been synonymous with visits from other planets. Therefore, the topic has been ridiculed, "believing" in UFOs is - well helped by Hollywood - being linked to believing in visitation of small green men from Mars in flying saucers, and in Norway it's almost social suicide to talk about the topic in public.

On the Internet, however, the topic is discussed relatively lively, - anonymously, - on both Norwegian and international discussion forums, so it is clear that there exist some interest in the topic, after all.

My interest in the subject was awakened in the early eighties. In 1981, some strange light phenomena appeared in the small mountain village of Hessdalen in Holtålen municipality, a few kilometers northwest of the town Røros in the middle Norway. This soon reached the newspapers, and all the reports led to "UFO fever" in Trøndelag in the early winter months of 1982.

Residents of Hessdalen didn't "only" see lights, however, eventually brave people living in Hessdalen appeared and told about "crafts" - with shapes like saucer and cigar, or eggs and triangles - these being so close that they had been able to throw stones at them. Many people from all around Norway went to Hessdalen to experience the phenomena themselves, while most people made up their minds based on how the matter became portrayed in the media. It wasn't lack of "explanations". Everything from reflection of car headlights from Støren village, or railway lights from Rørosbanen - to ball lightning or even the planet Mars floating through the valley, was presented as a "solution" - without exception by "experts" who had *not* visited Hessdalen and experienced the phenomena themselves.

Although I was only a little boy in 1981 - I remember the discussions at family gatherings, between those on the one hand who had confidence in the attempts at explanation that were served, and those on the other side who actually believed in the stories told by people living in Hessdalen. These discussions were often heated, and it made an impression on a little boy. What was all the fuss about?

The phenomena in Hessdalen persisted throughout the 1980s. In 1983, a group of enthusiasts started a research project - "Project Hessdalen" - hoping to find out more about the phenomena. They had partial support from universities, as well as the norwegian defense research institute, and therefore had access to advanced instruments such as a spectrum analyzer, magnetometer, radar, geiger counter, IR viewer etc. in a four-week field action carried out during January / February 1984. They did not succeed in finding the solution to the mystery, but at least they were able to kill all train light / car lights and planet theories.

I continued to hear about UFOs and Hessdalen during the 80s. The newspapers wrote about it at irregular intervals, and occasionally there were something on radio and TV. At one point, probably sometime in 1983 or 1984, I came - by "accident" - across a documentary program sent on NRK (Norwegian Broadcasting Corporation) that dealt with the UFO phenomenon. This program made an unforgettable impression on me. Among other things, a reconstruction was presented - in the form of a drawing of an "alien" - this was in connection with a testimony of a UFO abduction / kidnapping (or "close encounter of the 4th kind" as it's often called), and this type of creature was alleged to be pilots / crew on board the UFOs.

I can still picture the drawing; small creatures, with oversized, hairless, head in relation to the body. Big, black, slanted eyes - vicious looking. No ears, two small holes for a nose, and just a dash to a mouth. Long, thin arms, as well as flimsy, thin legs. This, along with pale gray-white skin, *did not* resemble a likeable exterior. I was almost traumatized by the vision, and I was afraid of the dark for a long time. The kidnapping in the TV show allegedly happened in the middle of the day, so I did not feel safe in daylight either...

My fear of the dark subsided as I grew up. The same happened for my interest in UFOs. In Hessdalen, fewer reports came in than in previous years, and the media coverage was limited to a few occasional articles now and then. My life was primarily about football, school and friends, as with teenage boys most, and a little later I started to go to parties and met my first girlfriend. UFOs was a peripheral thought. So it continued for several years, until the winter of 1993, the same year I graduated high school. I watched a TV-documentary series about UFOs and got renewed my curiosity about the subject.

In the autumn of 93 I started at the University in Trondheim, and within a few months I borrowed all of the books of the Trondheim public library that covered the UFO topic. Admittedly, that did not help studying for my exams, but eventually I saw more and more connections and patterns across data on UFO reports - which ultimately convinced me of the existence of the phenomenon.

The public library also had books about Hessdalen; "The UFO mystery in Hessdalen" by journalist Arne Wisth - 1983 - and "The UFO phenomenon - can the impossible be possible?" by auditor and hobby-ufolog Leif Havik, 1987. These books, with many reports and descriptions, showed me that what was seen by residents and visitors in Hessdalen in the 80s was exactly the same phenomenon - UFO - which is reportedinternationally, as I read about it in the books.

Later, there were studies for my part. I learned - among other things - about scientific method, and reliability, validity, - and *triangulation* , which means referring to observations using at least two different perspectives, according to wikipedia:

> "*By combining different perspectives one can uncover weaknesses in the perspectives separately. If the different perspectives point in different directions, then it indicates that the perspectives have bias, while if the perspectives point in the same direction, it may indicate that the results have high validity.* "*One way to achieve this is by using different datasets from different sources, times, locations and people.*

And that is precisely what one does when comparing reports from Hessdalen in the 80s with reports internationally, from different eras, - from the US, Australia, South America - etc.
The descriptions and patterns are relatively limited. It is the same shapes; disc, cigar /cylinder, oval / egg and triangle. The same pattern of movement and maneuvers; undulating motions, pendulum / spiral movements, - as well as abrupt, angular turns, zigzag patterns and more, - the same light compositions and colors. Descriptions of sounds are the same, and in the few cases where odor is registered, this also fits...

When multiple independent witnesses, separated geographically and in time and without the possibility of having mutual contact, largely give identical descriptions, down to a level of detail that indicates that it is absurd to blame it on coincidence. Everything suggests that what they are telling actually is true and genuine. The phenomenon and reports were - and are - not the result of misinterpretations, hallucinations and / or bluffs.

The UFO phenomenon came "abruptly" in Hessdalen in the 80s, and the people living in Hessdalen had not "read themselves up" on international literature on the phenomenon - which in addition was exclusively available in English at that time. Nevertheless, the people of Hessdalen - down to the last detail - described the same thing that has been reported
internationally.

So, I had been confirmed for my own part that the phenomenon was real, - UFOs in the sense of unknown vessels (ie NOT misinterpretations, hallucinations or bluffs, hitherto unknown geophysical Phenomena or meteorological phenomena) were real and they existed!

At this time, I was relatively convinced that UFOs represented something extraterrestrial. Ie that I considered the UFOs to be manned crafts from another solar system, - another planet. Alternatively, I'd look at UFOs as possible interdimensional vessels, or could it be time travelers?

However, my conclusions were in contrast to the latest development in Hessdalen. At this time, the project had been "revived", and in 1994 Project Hessdalen Workshop was held at Hessdalen community center, for a total of one week. Here, researchers and experts from various disciplines from all over the world participated - among others, the candidate for the Nobel Prize in Physics, Boris Smirnov. Various suggestions for explanatory models were presented. Most of them were based on the geophysical conditions in the areas in and around Hessdalen, which are rich in ore and various minerals. It was assumed that tensions arose, and that different energies and mechanisms led to light.

I was actually present at the last day of the week, which was less technical in the content, and therefore open to the public. Together with several of Hessdalen residents and other curious visitors, I got to hear a lecture by Leif Havik. At least as interesting as the lecture itself, was that during the break - in the parking lot outside the community center - I saw a light sphere rise over the horizon, stand still for a few seconds, then sink down behind the mountain again. My first UFO observation!

The organization "UFO-Norway" was also present this evening, and I grabbed the chance to sign up. As a paying member, the member magazine "UFO" dumped into my mailbox at irregular intervals. Here was a lot of interesting stuff, about both national and international UFO cases. What was not as good in my eyes, however, was the coverage of Hessdalen in the magazine, - and what was now consequently referred to as the "Hessdalen phenomenon".

They had stopped using the UFO definition when it came to

Hessdalen, and instead placed what was happening in a separate, isolated subcategory of the UFO phenomenon; a kind of hitherto unknown natural phenomenon or atmospheric light phenomenon. This accusation began to annoy me, because in my opinion it was a clear form of *under-reporting* . As I said, I had long since concluded that the UFO phenomenon in Hessdalen and the UFO phenomenon globally was exactly the same phenomenon, and certainly not separate things.

In 1998, an automatic measuring station was set up in Hessdalen. A blue container box was mounted up in Vårhuslia, with cameras connected to a computer rigged with software set to respond to light. When an "alarm" went off, a video recorder would start automatically.

Over the years, the "Blue Box" has become increasingly more advanced, with addition of several cameras, more instruments and more equipment. However, there have been many "false alarms"; airplanes, snowmobiles, insects, etc. - but the project team have also managed to capture genuinely unknown things, - which after thorough research, the researchers have still not been able to identify. Even though they have received more data, they have not succeeded in getting closer to a solution to the puzzle. - "The more data we get, the more mysterious it is," as project manager Erling Strand said.

Italian Massimo Teodorani, a doctor of astrophysics, was present at the workshop in Hessdalen in 1994. In the late 90s and in the early 2000s he was leader of, and chairing, Project EMBLA, which eventually became an Italian branch of project Hessdalen. The EMBLA team carried out three field actions over three years in Hessdalen, and a number of analyzes and several articles were published. Teodorani & co's starting point, was that the phenomena in Hessdalen were related to the geophysical conditions, and that luminous plasma arose as a result of tension in the bedrock. But Teodorani also maintained that a small but significant minority of the observed and recorded phenomena - were *not* having plasma characteristics, but were marked by being illuminated, solid objects.

Teodorani was also involved in the SETV project; Search for

Extraterrestrial Visitation, which was based on the idea that the globe, among other things - in places like Hessdalen - could be visited by possible self-reproducing "robotic probes", - a type of advanced extraterrestrial drones, and eventually included this hypothesis in several of his analyzes and articles.

This was an interesting read, I thought - and made a new impression on my thinking about UFOs and Hessdalen. Teodorani further maintained that although the observed and photographed lights in Hessdalen had *outer* plasma-like characteristics, this did not necessarily mean that the phenomena were exclusively plasma, transverse, below the surface and into the center. On the contrary, there was not enough advanced photo-technical equipment available to make an assessment of what was *below the* surface. In other words; what was photographed could just as well be solid objects, made of metal, - *surrounded* by an outer layer of plasma.

In the summer of 2007, the media announced that the "mystery" in Hessdalen was resolved. In an episode on NRK's "Summer open" programme, an employee at Østfold University, who is also involved in Science Camp and affiliated with the research projects in Hessdalen, was interviewed - where the person launched a theory of what is happening. Easily said; there was dust from the ground in Hessdalen which was ignited and through a combustion process caused light. These lights moved around the valley with the wind. However, the theory did not take into account that "dust from the ground" is often covered by several meters of deep snow for much of the year, for example - which is just *one* of the problems with the theory...

However, people involved with the research program quickly went out and denied that they had any solution to the phenomena. On the contrary, it was emphasized that one got conflicting data, that the phenomenon was more complex than assumed, and that one might be farther away from a solution than ever before. Nevertheless, it seems that some part of the public opinions are left with the impression that the mystery *is* solved, and if you google UFO + Hessdalen, Adresseavisen's (Trondheims newspaper) article from 2007 with the headline "The UFO-mystery solved in Hessdalen" listed as the first hit.

Eventually, I came across a new approach to the topic - *beyond the* unknown natural phenomenon hypothesis, and the ET- hypothesis, additionally those who claim that the UFO phenomenon is "man-made" - that is, man-made technology hidden from the public. There are a number of different variations of these theories, but many of them have a background in the idea of technology developed in Nazi Germany and later imported into the United States as part of "operation paperclip" and then further developed in secret, black military projects.

Another version goes in lines of Nazi "survival" where the same technology has been further developed in South America, preferably Argentina, by refugee Nazi engineers and scientists, and that during the Cold War there existed a type of "third power" next to the East and West - a kind of *Nazi international* who operated in secret and had acquired position, power and influence through superior technology.

The extreme variant of these theories advocates Nazi UFO bases in Antarctica, and even on the moon!

The more moderate claim is that there exists an internationally fascist, hidden, interterritorial network that controls and overrides governments and disposes technology withdrawn from the public.

Little by little I began to ponder whether Hessdalen and the phenomena could be placed in a similar scenario. I found that there was a NATO base south of Hessdalen, at mount Hummelfjell, and an other smaller NATO base north of Hessdalen, at mount Bringen. Between these mountain peaks there are nine miles, - along the Hessdalen valley. These bases were radar observatories, as part of NATO's control and warning systems (the KOGV system) during the Cold War. Could it be that a top-secret branch of NATO conducted exotic technology experimentation in a deserted area like Hessdalen, with or without help of the Norwegian army?

The idea was specious, but it also raised many problems. What about the personnel at these bases? At most, there were one hundred employees at the base at mount Hummelfjell. Would it be possible to keep something like that secret? Wouldn't anyone have spoken out? The more people involved in a conspiracy, the harder it is to keep it secret. Or did they operate on a need-to-know basis, so that only a few knew?

The already mentioned Teodorani wrote something similar in one of his articles about Hessdalen:

> *"On the contrary it is even more reasonable to suspect that the governments which are at present possibly experimenting flying devices working with "exotic technology", would choose locations just like Hessdalen in order to work with no disturb by putting into practice the best of the camouflages. The co-existence of anomalous lights of possible natural origin linked to the territory and of flying machines born from some mind of the "Skunk Works" might permit to some government to operate in total secret by letting the public opinion believe that Hessdalen is a alien basis."(The Physical Study of Atmospheric Luminous Anomalies and the SETV Hypothesis, 2002).*

However, there is several problems with such a theory; firstly, - the light phenomena (whether they have geophysical origin or not) arose at about the same time as what was described as *vessels* during the daytime ("daylight discs") - ie from December 1981 and throughout the winter 1982. So it was not that something "skunk works"-like "chose" Hessdalen as a location to test exotic "planes" because of an *already* existing occurrence of unknown natural phenomena in the area, that could act as a "smokescreen". Thus, the hypothesis does not match the timeline. Secondly, it would be very strange if experimentation with exotic technology persisted beyond the 80s - yes, right up to the present - considering the attention Hessdalen has been, and still are being, devoted in norwegian and international media. Why not move the experiment to another and more anonymous and undisturbed location? *Finnmarksvidda* (far northern Norway), for example, would probably have been just as natural? And by the way; will they never finish this experimentation?

On the other hand; - if some kind of "visitation" is the alternative; - interstellar space travel requires advanced technology. Technology that far exceeds our capacity, and which will manifest itself as sci-fi in the foreseeable future. Does the reported observation material - in the form of metallic looking crafts - with "nuts and bolts" - represent sufficiently advanced technology?

Apparently, the described UFOs resemble our planes, rockets and satellites – decades ahead in development. In one case in Hessdalen, for example, the observer describes that the object "was clearly composed of metal plates". Wouldn't you expect anything far more exotic if "guests" from another solar system, or even another galaxy - thousands - yes, maybe millions of years ahead of us in development?

It can be visitors from a "different dimension", someone who wants to invade - a "parallel world". But the same argument still holds, will I maintain? And if you go on about "dimensions" etc., it requires a whole new physique. The same applies to the theory of UFOs as time travelers, ie. visitors from our own future.

So I wavered between a number of theories, "explanations" and "models" on the UFO phenomenon without getting closer to a solution I could settle with; The natural phenomena theories were insufficient, and it was not difficult to find large gaps and deficiencies in BOTH the "manmade" hypothesis AND the various "visitation" theories. I was stuck ...

However, what I felt (and still feel) quite *certain* about, was that Hessdalen represents the UFO phenomenon "in miniature"; - implicit that almost everything that is reported internationally in the UFO context is *also* reported in Hessdalen one or more times. The UFO phenomenon in Hessdalen and the UFO phenomenon globally must therefore be regarded as the *same* phenomenon. And a solution to the UFO mystery in Hessdalen will thus represent a solution to the UFO phenomenon as a whole.

2 TRIP TO SWEDEN AND A PIT STOP

In the summer of 2017, at the end of July / August, my fiance - Hege - and I sat on the internet and searched for airline tickets and hotel places etc. We had been busy with some projects in the garden, as well as renovation of the house, among other things, and have not planned any holiday so far. We are therefore late, so there's not much to choose from. What we prefer - of course - costs a fortune. After much back and forth we agree to drop the idea of airline tickets and instead take the car to Sweden, drive around and stay in different hotels. The weather is nice, sunny and warm, and with the car available we're flexible and can drive where the sun shines.

We pack our suitcases and leave. We have decided to drive via Røros, across the border to Sweden, through Fünesdalen and further towards Sveg. Then south to Mora. On our way up to Røros we will pass Hessdalen. I have mentioned my UFO interest, and told a little about Hessdalen and the phenomena there. We have also seen some of the documentary films about Hessdalen that are online. Hege thinks this is exciting, and when I suggest that we can take a quick visit to the valley, she is not at all hard to convince.

Hessdalen is located in Holtålen municipality, northwest of Røros. Driving up Valley Gauldalen, you pass the exit to Hessdalen just before Ålen, which is the administration center in the municipality. The exit up Hessdalslia Hill is new. Previously, it came as a surprise after a curve, and I had to brake heavily. A new sign has also come up; The "Hessdalen phenomenon", it says - with a landmark symbol. I'm not sure if I like it ... All good that the phenomenon finally are recognized, but not to isolate Hessdalen as a type of subcategory of the UFO phenomenon - or worse - try to distance events in Hessdalen away from the UFO phenomenon.

The UFO flap in Hessdalen is the world's largest UFO wave. No other place in the world has so many UFOs been observed over such a long period of time. And this wave is still going on! It is therefore not to be denied that it tickles slightly in the stomach through the steep and winding road up the hill to Hessdalen.

The Hessdalen valley is a mountain village, and the view you get to see when you arrive at the top, the valley and the mountains that surround it in front of you, takes your breath away.

A new thing, is that they have established a parking lot at Hessdalskjølen and have set up information boards regarding the phenomenon intended for tourists. Strictly speaking, we are on vacation - and thus tourists by definition - so we leave the car and allow us to read.

The boards present some of the history, - how the observations started in December 1981, and came into the media's spotlight throughout the winter of 1982. How Project Hessdalen was founded in 1983. About the field actions in 84 and 85. The revitalization of the project in the 90s and developments since then against today.

Besides, it says a bit about what one can have the opportunity to see. The phenomena can be divided into different categories, it says. The first category is white or blue flashes of light that last from less than a second up to a few seconds. Often, several such flashes can be seen one after the other. The second category consists of light-colored or ellipse-shaped lights, which can stand still or move around - sometimes with accelerated speeds, while the third category deals with several lights that follow each other so it seems that the lights may be attached to an object. Occasionally, something dark or black is seen between these lights. The lights can have different colors, it says on the board.

After we're finished reading, we cross the road and drive through the forest up to Aspåskjølen. This is really a bit of a cult place, I say to Hege. In the 80's, dozens of cars could often park here, and hundreds of people could be gathered in the evenings scouting for the UFOs.

Aspåskjølen. Mount Finnsåhøgda in the background.

It was at this place Project Hessdalen was headquartered during the field action in 1984. A caravan was placed in the middle of Aspåskjølen, supplied with electricity through several hundred meters of cable down to the nearest farm, and equipped with radar, magnetometer, spectrum analyzer, geiger counter and various other borrowed equipment. No solution was found, but several theories could be sorted out, and were rejected.

Aspåskjølen itself is located at an altitude of 700 meters. Right in front lies the mountain Finnsåhøgda. One could often see the UFOs pass between Aspåskjølen and Finnsåhøgda, with the mountain in the background; - the low altitude, course changes, as well as the fact that the UFOs occasionally stopped and stood still - or rushed off at tremendous speed, - and that no sound could be heard - excluded aircraft, helicopter or other conventional aircrafts.

When it was at the most frequent, it also came to almost fixed times - to the extent that one was talking about the "half past seven-flight", or
"half past ten-flight ...

Various shapes were seen; cigar-shaped - or as a fuselage without wings, like a projectile – or a pistol bullet, rounded at one end and pointed at the other. Sometimes the phenomena were seen during the day, - so-called daylight observations, and in some cases so close the observer could throw stones at them. In the most intense period one could see the phenomenon several times a day. It went so far that courageous residents in Hessdalen began to discuss the possibility of shooting down some of the crafts, and also initiated a petition where the claim was that public authorities had to initiate investigations. List of signatures was delivered to the police office in Holtålen. "The UFOs reported to the police" was the headline in the newspapers...

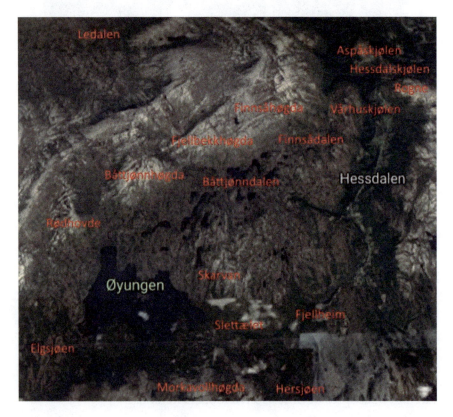

We drive the approximately 12 kilometers through the valley. It's only around 200 resident here. We pass the community center and the old grocery store, which is now closed. A few rusty petrol pumps are all that remains of the gas station. We pass the church, and further into the valley, the disused school. There are many dilapidated houses and abandoned farms. Up in the hillside, on the other side of the river, we see the now uninhabited farm "Finnsåvollen". According to the old guest book on the Project Hessdalen website, an Oslo couple in their twenties apparently saw a UFO landing here when they came driving after the Hessdalen road a winter evening around the middle of the 90s. The object was supposed to have been as big as the main house on the farm and flashed in all colors like a Christmas tree. The couple made their way to the farm the following day, and apparently found imprints in the snow, - both after the UFO and some kind of "footprints" next to them...

By the end of the road, we turn and drive the same way back. Up in Vårhuslia Hill we see "Blue Box" where the cameras that broadcast live on the internet are mounted. It stands on the ground of Bjarne Lillevold. Bjarne is one of those who have seen most UFOs of the residents, and is interviewed in several of the documentary films we have seen. He can be an example of the typical Hessdalen resident; down to earth, calm, trustworthy and reliable. Only once has he been scared during an observation, he says:

- If I had hair on my head, it would have risen!

Otherwise, he is not particularly easily scared, we notice. Under the tab "latest observations" on the Project Hessdalen homepage you can read about Bjarnes preliminary last experience:

Date: 22.08.2017 **Time:** 01:30 (at night) **Location:** Vårhus, Hessdalen. **Observer:**
Bjarne Lillevold

Bjarne saw a bright green light, which illuminated the entire northern part of Vårhusgrenda. It shone for approx. 3 minutes before it turned off. Bjarne thought it was a bit scary with this green light that lit up a large area.

Understandable...!

Bjarne has nearly 100 observations, he says in Terje Toftnes documentary film about Hessdalen, "The Portal". - And everything is written down, says Bjarne.

I would have liked to have a look at that notebook!

After this sightseeing, we set course for Sweden. Along the way, we continue to discuss UFOs and Hessdalen. It seems that Hege has taken a stronger interest in the subject now that she has seen the place with her own eyes.

3 A GLIMPSE OF THE PHENOMENON

Over the autumn we're increasingly talking about taking a trip to Hessdalen. Different circumstances prevents us from going, - right up to November, we filed a large thermos with black coffee, get in the Mitsubishi and set course up the Gauldalen Valley.

In the time that has passed since the summer holidays, we have followed the Project Hessdalen website a bit. There have been some observations. Among others, one under "science camp" now in September - done by the project manager himself, Erling Strand. Strand became aware of a large light over Vårhuskjølen. Later, the light moved through the valley, to the south. Strand took his car and drove towards the light. People he met south in the valley confirmed that they had also seen the phenomenon.

In an interview on the local radio station, NEA radio, he states that the light was of such a character, that it gave him associations to the 80s, - crafts and vehicles, etc.

However, on the trip upwards, we talk mostly about everyday things. Jobs, kids and home etc. My expectations are not that great. Well, there have been observations lately, but I consider the chance for us to be lucky enough to see something *now*, as minimal.

It was in the 80's they did see lights every day. Up to 20-30 observations a week. Now it is, according to the Project Hessdalen website, down to 20 - 30 observations per year. This may just as well be because people do not report anymore, but still... Hege's expectations are hard to determine. She probably has no expectations at all.

A thermos of coffee later, we pass the sign that says Hessdalen and head up the steep Hessdalen hillside. As we approach the top, - Hessdalskjølen, - I think of a youtube clip with Ruth Mary Moe talking about an experience she had while driving a car right here;

> *"there was something that went over the car. It was like an enlightened gentleman hat. Everything was lit up as in the middle of the day. The forest and Mount Rogne... it was weird, I tell you. You drive in the dark, and suddenly everything is illuminated around you..."*

Ruth Mary lived at one of the three farms below Aspåskjølen and was one of the very first residents of Hessdalen who became aware of the weird lights that flew by first in the 80's. She was furthermore fearless and outspoken. "We don't see just light," she said. We see hulls as well... Ruth Mary was honest, and did not hold back in interviews and in the media. And this made problems for her: "We were terribly ridiculed. At one time it was difficult to go down to Ålen Village to the supermarket because of all the jokes and fun making!"

We turn right at the Red Cross cabin and drive the few hundred meters through the forest up on Aspåskjølen, and park the car in the direction of Finnsåhøgda. Panorama view! Perfect! Then, - wait... A farmer is doing some work with some hay balls. Eventually he becomes aware of us, leave what he has in his hands and comes up the hill with long steps. I roll down the window and say hello, a little cautiously.

- Do you need help?
No, we just want to stay here and...
- Sorry, this is private ground. You can't stay here! Drive down to the Red Cross cabin. Your view is just as good from there.

Uh... ok...! I've parked here before, and never heard of anyone who has been chased from here. On the contrary, people in Hessdalen are known for their hospitality. In the 80's it even happened that frozen

UFO hunters were served both coffee and fresh waffles by the residents at the farms below, including Ruth Mary.

We obey and drive down to the Red Cross cabin. From there, however, we can't see a thing due to the forest, so we turn into the parking lot with the information boards on the other side of the road instead. From here we have pretty good view, after all.

The before mentioned Bjarne Lillevold had a particularly interesting observation right here in the early 80s. He came up Hessdalslia Hill riding on a moped, after finishing work, and saw a light up on the top of the hill. He first thought it was the Red Cross cabin that was on fire. When he came up to Hessdalskjølen, however, he saw that it was a craft; it looked like a Christmas tree upside down and it went up and down like a jojo while it made a hissing sound. There was a kind of woolly coating around the object, and it looked like it radiated heat of some kind.

The story goes that Bjarne - supposedly - according to an article at the National Organization UFO Sweden's website (ufo.se) afterwards became aware that the time had gone so fast...

> *"From the place where I first saw the UFO to my home, it is 5- 10 minutes drive. When I last saw the UFO was at 11pm and I came home half past midnight. What I did in the last 90 minutes I don't remember. I know that I was at the observation site and that I went home, but I cannot account for what happened at the site. A memory gap exists here.*
>
> *I talked to a psychologist about it. He suggested that I may have been inside the UFO, but I objected to that, because I have no memory of such a thing."*

The sighting is mentioned both in Wisth's and Havik's books, but the part with "lost time" is not mentioned. The Swedish article is authored by Clas Svahn who is experienced in the UFO field and has a good reputation. It would have been interesting to hear Bjarne tell about this himself in his own words. Bjarne lives on the farm right below "Blue Box" at Vårhus, just about one kilometer away...

I have to go out of the car in a necessary errand and read a little on the boards about the various categories. Again it strikes me that these descriptions are almost on the verge of underreporting. The focus is solely on light. The fact that solid objects are seen as well, even in daylight, is barely mentioned...

Another categorization than the one on the info boards can be found in Arne Wisth's book, "The UFO mystery in Hessdalen", 1983:

> *"We can confirm that at least four different types of UFOs are involved:" The Observation-UFO "which is round or ovoid. The "hat", which has the classic flying saucer shape. "The Pistol Bullet", which is pointed at one end and rounded in the other, which often stands still for long periods and also lands. "The Cigar" - which is big, maybe a hundred meters long or more".*

It is something like that we would like to see, but first and foremost we just hope to see "something "- anything, really.

It's a fine November night, starlit and minus five degrees. To my surprise and joy, I notice that Hege is at least as eager as me. She constantly exclaims: "There!?" and points. No. It's a plane..."

Yes, there is constant air traffic, we see. But we quickly get used to it and recognize with ease the composition of lights and the characteristic way they flash. Besides, the sound from the motors is easy to hear. Reflections on a road sign nearby when car lights are passing fools us almost a couple of times, then it is quiet. Mount Finnsåhøgda is dark and towering in front of us. Suddenly! THERE! "Did you see it? !!?" Illumination over a large area a few seconds, - an intensely blue-and-white light, like an explosion - but without sound. Then the sky is dark again, and everything is quiet and calm. Inside the car, however, it is anything but quiet! "Did you see that?! "DID YOU SEE IT?!" Yes, we both saw it. What is communicated the next few minutes, I'm unsure of. But especially meaningful and sensible, it hardly is. We're staring intensely at the horizon of Finnsåhøgda, hardly dare to blink ...

After five to ten minutes - a new fiery flash of light - in the same place - even more powerful than the last time. The color is again blue-white ... it reminds us of a powerful bomb or gigantic dynamite charge. Afterwards, everything is normal. We sit for another hour, hoping to see something more, but finally decide to think about the way home. After all, it's a long drive, and it's getting late. We still want to see more, but after all we have actually seen SOMETHING. And it made an impression! It's just miles of miles with uninhabited wilderness behind Finnsåhøgda. It wasn't lightning. There were hardly any clouds in the sky, this is inexplicable!

We discuss eagerly on the way home. What do we think about this? We are unable to find any explanation. When we got home, - on youtube, we find a film that also shows powerful flashes of light over Mount Finnsåhøgda, almost the same as we saw, and almost in the same place. The difference is just that what we saw was even more powerful. For Hege, this only has made her want to see more. There is something inexplicable in Hessdalen, and we saw it with our own eyes! We agree ... we must get back to Hessdalen right away!

4 "15 METERS"

However, Christmas passes until we manage to go back to Hessdalen. This time, however, we have bad luck with the weather. There is dense snow, and the visibility is bad. Useless to try to observe anything under such conditions, so we drive back home after a couple of rather wasted hours. Miss!

However, we don't give up that easy, and instead start looking online for lodging in the area. I have a few days off from work, and the first week in March we have rented a cabin for two days south in Hessdalen.

We arrive in Hessdalen early in the afternoon. The cabin is located at Jenshaugen, just beside a parking lot for snowmobiles, south in the valley. I recognize the area from a NRK documentary on youtube. In one of the episodes, a married Trondheim couple is interviewed with "our" cabin in the background. Asked if they have seen any UFOs, they reluctantly admit that "yes, they have" - a saucer, like the kids draw, they tell, with a dome on top and lights around...

The reporter makes a big number out of the fact that he is "talking with urban people now", and therefore he had expected them to be "sober" - as he puts it. Quite illustrative of the attitude, and with the tone a NRK employee could allow himself in this era, and still get away with!

The cabin owner, Tor Moen, stops by and say hello. We talk about the terrain and skiing opportunities nearby. Then he asks if we've come to look for UFOs? We must confirm that, even if it feels uncomfortable to say it out loud. Then we talk a little about observations done in Hessdalen lately, as well as the research and a bit about the different theories. Tor would like to hear what we think. He himself does not say much about what he has seen...

The following day we go to Tor's son-in-law, who lives at the neighboring farm, to fill up our water tank. There is not much water in the cabin-well, as it has not been degrees above zero this winter. He takes a quick look at us and asks quite simply; "UFO?" It begins to dawn on me that in Hessdalen, UFOs is an everyday topic of conversation, and it gradually begins to feel more natural to talk about it.

After unpacking, we go for a ride in the terrain towards Øyongen. The scooter tracks are hard as asphalt, so we leave the skis in the car and go by foot. I've not been to this area before. I didn't know it was so hilly, and at times so steep, it looks flat on the map...

It was in this area that a cabin owner - according to the rumors - worked with woodcutting by snowmobile. While he was working, he got aware that something was over him. He looked up, and then looked straight at the rim on a flying, round construction that hung silently just above the treetops. He described it as the classic flying saucer type. Soon after, it moved silently across the forest. It took over a week before he got to sleep properly. The shock was apparent.

--

In the evening we drive up to Aspåskjølen. We park in the forest and walk the last few meters by foot. Since last time we have acquired insulated coveralls, so now we should be well equipped both against the wind and the cold. The farmer can't deny us to stand on the road, right? It's a public road, so...

It's something completely different to stand outdoors in the open air, we notice. The overview is far better this way compared to the car.

Aspåskjølen is a large, open area. We don't see the lights from the three farms below Aspåskjølen from where we stand, and it is far to the settlement inside the valley. One really feels quite small when standing outdoors in the winter night with a starry sky above us. It is quiet and peaceful. Not a sound, other than from a plane passing over us now and then.

While I'm standing with my back turned to it, Hege sees a flash of light. Not big and powerful, just like what we saw the last time in November, but small and concentrated. - As a flashlight that quickly turns on and off, Hege said. The light is below the edge of Vårhuskjølen - that is, below the horizon, with the mountain as a background.

I've read about this; There are two types of flashes that are often reported: Large and powerful ones that illuminate large parts of the sky, and small, concentrated, pointed flashes. There are no settlements, cabins or roads in the area, and people out in the deep snow at that place at this time is very unlikely.

We have a small flashlight ourselves. We point it in the direction of Vårhuskjølen and turn it off and on several times in succession. In the 80's, it was reported that if a strong light source was aimed - such as car lights, heavy flashlight etc. - in the direction of the phenomena - they responded; for example, by flashing, disappearing, etc. Our pocket flashlight, however, cost 100,- NOK. at the supermarket down in Ålen and does not qualify for a strong light source. Nothing happens.

The next day we want to get a better view. We drive up to Hessdalskjølen and take the skis up to Mount Rogne. There is a lot of fresh loose snow, and the sweat is pouring from us before we find a suitable place to sit midway up the mountain side with usable wind shielding. Here, however, we have a fantastic view over the entire front part of Hessdalen. We light a bonfire and take out the thermos with coffee while looking for any phenomena.

So-called daylight observations are rare in Hessdalen, as in general in UFO context. Most often, night lights are reported - also in

Hessdalen. Occasionally - especially in the 80's - phenomena have been reported during the day. Then it's no longer talk of light, - you're able to see a solid object. A craft made of metal in different shapes. It's something like that we hope to see, where we sit.

In the heat of the fire it is quite comfortable inside the coverall, but except for the magnificent nature, there is little to report about for our part.

We believe that it would be very interesting to meet some of the residents in Hessdalen. Talk to them and hear what they have to tell. Before we left, there was a TV broadcast from Hessdalen. The program "Norway - now!" sent live from the UFO camp in Vårhus. Here was both Erling Strand and several resident interviewed - including Jon Arvid Aspås, who is one of those who have seen most in Hessdalen ever since 1981. In the TV show, Jon Arvid says:

> *"... it's almost just to make fun of the population in the valley here when the researchers talk about gas coming up from the earth and the like. I have seen it many times myself, and I know with certainty that it is a solid vehicle - a craft!"*

Jon Arvid seems like a nice guy. Earlier this day I found his phone number on the internet, as well as his address. Hege suggests sending him a polite SMS and asking if he has time to meet us and tell a little about it. No sooner said than done. Immediately afterwards, Jon Arvid is on the line and says that he has both time and opportunity. Just stop by anytime. We agree that we will come after we are down from the mountain. We stop by the cabin and put on clothes that don't smell of bonfire.

Jon Arvid lives at Hegseth approximately in the middle of the valley. We knock on the door, and Jon Arvid gestures from the living room window that we just can go straight in. Immediately afterwards, we're sitting on the couch of the man who has probably seen UFOs most times, not just here in Hessdalen - but perhaps also on a worldwide basis?!

- I've stopped counting, but at least I've seen *it* over a hundred times…

Jon Arvid asks a little about who we are and where we come from, and what we do for a living. Then he asks how long we have been sitting up there in the mountainside on Mount Rogne.

It's difficult to get to see it in the daytime, he says. - Are you going to be here for two days? If you had been here for two *years* you might have seen it! What was here in the 80's - vehicles, crafts, etc. - is more or less gone in my opinion. It's been a few years since the last time I saw it myself.

We tell about the powerful flashes of light we saw in November over Mount Finnsåhøgda, and the less powerful flash Hege saw towards Vårhuskjølen last night.

- Yeah. We see these flashes of light all the time. These are the ones the scientists are analyzing.

- Yes, but don't you think that the light flashes and the crafts are two sides of the same phenomenon, we ask?

- It may be. We talked about it already in the 80s, that maybe there was a connection. Several times we saw flashes ahead of an observation… I think the researchers are astray. It is no burning gas or plasma that causes these lights. In the 80s, for example, when we stood up on Aspåskjølen in the evenings, we saw on several occasions that the lights dimmed and extinguished when a plane passed over. When the plane had passed, the light turned on again. Who on earth was up there and lit up the "gas" again? No, I don't think they'll find out what it is. But if they are to find out, in time for me to know, then they have to start hurrying… I'm starting to become an old man. I turned 82 years a month ago… We wouldn't have thought so! He looks much younger, we must say!

Maybe it's the fresh mountain air, and skiing in the mountains that keeps him healthy? Jon Arvid says that in the 80s it became almost like an obsession for him to see it as many times as possible. He set off for skiing in the mountains, at night, to get as close as possible.

- On a few occasions I have been approx. 15 meters from "it". One time it happened here; Jon Arvid points out the living room window, - over the roof of the barn. The second time was on a trip from Ålen to Tydal. We were going to pick up a snowmobile and stood in a parking lot as it suddenly passed straight over our heads.

- How did it look up close?

It looked strange! The hull looked like a radiator on the underside - there were some kind of pipes there ... and three "paws" - landing feet. This is probably the only time I've heard a slight sound from the machinery on it. It sounded like a badly lubricated bicycle chain.

Jon Arvid tells stories about UFOs seen on both short and longer hold. He usually tells about his own experiences. Other people's observations he is more reluctant to tell about.

He talked about a scooter trip in 1982 to Ledalen Valley, - behind Finnsåhøgda. - It was said that the lights landed there.

- There were me and two buddies who left. We drove the snowmobiles for an hour, and what we did see? I still recall as yesterday. There were three egg-shaped, luminous objects that stood in the air in front of us and hovered. Suddenly they changed positions. The middle light went straight up in the air, and immediately after, a light came from outside and occupied the space that the first object had left. Then we knew what we saw!

The moon was up this night. One of the objects flew over us in such an angle that we could see the moon reflecting in the metal on it ... It was as if they had radio connection to each other. On the ground, beneath the objects, there were small lights - as if there were some short "creatures" who jumped around with headlamps or something ... One of my buddies had just bought snowmobile, so we had to stop and wait for him when we drove into Ledalen. On the return trip, however, it was he who drove first. Then there was no hold back of speed ...! I wasn't that brave myself either. That night I didn't sleep!

- Have you ever been scared? No, says Jon Arvid, and leans forward in the chair. - Never scared. This is nothing dangerous, - had this been dangerous, then we would experience it now after so many years ...

- At first, in the 80s, we wondered if it could be anything military. The observations started at the same time as the new facility for the Home Guard was built in Haltdalen. One were wondering if there could be a connection ...

- But you no longer think so? - that this is something military?
 - No. Had there been a military force on earth that had this technology, then all warfare would have ended. It would be lasting peace!

There was a lady who lived down by Stensli, at the bottom of Hessdalslia Hill, at the exit from the national road. She was awake in the middle of the night - this was a hot summer night, in 1984 I think - and she couldn't sleep. She looked up towards the top of the Rogne Mountain, and saw a luminous object shaped like an oblong pistol bullet. Eventually, the object sunk down to the ground and landed. Through binoculars she saw a creature outside the craft, short and with long arms. The creature made some jumping movements around the object and then went back into it again. Afterwards, the object rose to the air, flattened, and departed.

Later that year, we were a few people that went up on the top of Rogne. We had radio connection with her, and she directed us to the place she thought the object had landed. At the spot we found imprints after three "paws". There was obviously something heavy that had stood there. The imprints were visible a long time afterwards...

- Have you seen it in daylight?

- I've seen it most as lights in the night, but in the 80s we saw it during the day as well. It was usually early in the morning one could get to see it. It could almost seem like they were flying north in the evening, and then came back in the morning, passing south.

Jon Arvid makes an errand in the bookshelf, comes back with the "UFO mystery" by journalist Arne Wisth published in 1983 and scrolls up the picture pages in the book.

- Sadly, they are not of good quality. In the 80's there was no one in Hessdalen, which had proper photo equipment, unfortunately. It's a shame there aren't any better pictures ...

When I hear Jon Arvid talk, I recognize the descriptions in international UFO books I've read. It's a striking match, and for me this is yet another indication of the reality of the UFO phenomenon and that Jon Arvid and other Hessdalen residents speak the truth. I tell Jon Arvid this, also.

Jon Arvid: "I know with 100% certainty that it is a solid vehicle - a craft!"

Even though we would like to stay longer and hear more, we thank him for coffee and cakes, the talk - and that he spent his time. It has been two interesting hours. I've read about some of his observations in books, and seen everything that there is of documentary films about Hessdalen. Jon Arvid is interviewed in several of them. Yet there is something different to hear it from him directly.

As he says: - I was so damn stupid that I started talking about this. Now I just have to continue ...

Before we go, we also mention that we would like to return to Hessdalen in the Easter vacation, if we find a cabin for rent, and that we might be talking again then?

At dusk we're in place on Aspåskjølen. The weather is ok, cold, but not starlit unfortunately. We stay for quite some time, but don't see anything sensational.

On the way back to the cabin, Hege sees a large, green flash in an arch over the sky - ahead of the car. It is Hege who drives, and she brakes. I look in another direction and don't see anything.

Hege is tired and wants to go inside the cabin and warm herself. I'll stay out a little more. I remember having read about an observation that happened here at Jenshaugen. A lady was waiting for the bus one early February morning in 1983. But it wasn't the bus that came; - Instead, a 15-meter silver-colored "rocket-like" object passed in front of her. The speed was low - until the object suddenly made a "loop" over the ridge and disappeared out of sight ...

Tonight neither buses nor "rockets" pass, and I go inside the cabin as well.

The next day, Jon Arvid calls. He may know about a cabin we can rent during the Easter holidays. - So, he wonders if we can stop by before we leave? We do so. The neighbor of Jon Arvid has a cabin that has been empty for some time. We can borrow it in the Easter if we want. You bet! Phone numbers are exchanged, and thus the Easter holidays are booked!

5 EASTER IN HESSDALEN

We arrive at Hessdalen a bit late in the morning on Wednesday 28th March. The cabin we've borrowed is located at Hegseth, - a couple of hundred meters below Jon Arvid's house. A good old-fashioned traditional Norwegian cabin, just as we hoped for. It has no running water. Because of that, we have to bring our own water. I get wood from the shed and pack
the stove full.

After unpacking, we go to Finnsådalen Valley on foot. Apart from some animal tracks and an absolutely magnificent nature, we see little of significance here, but it's great.

Back at the cabin we warm ourselves a little in front of the fireplace, and then drive up to Aspåskjølen around 9 o'clock. We park in the forest and walk the last few meters by foot. The snow crunches as we walk through it. It's almost full moon, minus 10 degrees and completely starlit.

Almost immediately I notice something I suppose is a plane high in the sky inside the main part of Hessdalen itself. This seems to take course in our direction, but after four to five seconds, it suddenly becomes weaker and then completely gone. Strange! Unfortunately, Hege does not see this as she stands with her back to it. It all goes so fast that I'm not sure what I've seen, but It wasn't a plane, but maybe a meteor or a satellite?

A while later, we both turn around at the same time - and see two bright spots vertically, one over and one under, which shines much stronger than the stars around in the north-east direction. We look at this for a few seconds, then both lights become weaker and disappear simultaneously, - completely synchronous! We have a certain feeling that the lights are lamps and not stars. I'm uncertain, but also believe that they slowly move parallelly in the direction away from us. Have the lights passed right over us ?! Anyway, we've got something to ponder on... Since there were two lights, and BOTH disappeared equally – completely synchronously - we can forget both meteors and satellites.

Back at the cabin we ask ourselves if we can also forget about gas and plasma theories; for can any natural phenomenon behave like this? Can such a thing occur by itself and occur at random in nature? It takes time to fall asleep this evening.

The next day, Thursday morning, we go up to Stordalshøgda mountain above Hegseth. Fantastic view from the top to the south, west and north. But it's so windy it's hard to stand upright. Instead we seek shelter a bit down the mountain side with our thermos and our coffee cups. From here, Hege sees a flash against the horizon of Finnsåhøgda.

At nine o'clock, we jump into the coveralls again, and drive up to Aspåskjølen. We park in the same place, and again it's clear and starry. After a while we spot a star far inside the valley. No - the "star" moves, so we assume it's an airplane. The light moves from west to east, apparently across Båttjønndalen valley. After a while, it seems to be turning, and the course then becomes more oblique over Vårhuskjølen in the direction of mount Rogne. We see that it's a constant yellow-white light, and no flashing plane-light is visible! In addition, it seems to be significantly lower than regular airplane altitude, and the distance from us to the light cannot be great? No sound can be heard.

As the light approaches Rogne, I'm curious about whether it will pass between us and Rogne, or whether it will disappear behind the mountain, - this could possibly tell about the distance from us to the light, and thus say something about the size of it - but before this becomes applicable, the light suddenly becomes weaker, and completely disappears within a few seconds, - just like the last few seconds before a light bulb burns out. The light "vibrates" in a way before it goes out ... What the... ?!

We see several flashes, including one I think is red, a little to the left of mount Rogne. The cold chases us back to the car, and we drive south in the valley to warm ourselves. Shortly after, on the stretch between Kjølen and Vårhus, - where you look down into the deep valley between Vårhuskjølen and Aspåskjølen, Hege sees an enormous light in front of mount Finnsåhøgda. It only takes a few seconds, then it's gone. I'm braking, but unfortunately just too late to see the light. The distance is hard to estimate, but she says "in the middle of the valley". It was a yellow-white round shape that was approx. twice the size of the moon.

This shocks her seriously. The light reminded her of the moon, Hege says, and since it is almost full moon, she speculates that it may have been a reflex of the moon she has seen.

The moon is at this time in the south-east. We check the next day if anything exists in the area that could have reflected the moon, - for example solar panel on the roof of a cabin etc. - but without luck.

We continue to the toll road at Fjellheim, turn and drive north again to Aspåskjølen. Hege is still shook up after the experience with the big light, and doesn't really want to stay outside. It's windy and bitterly cold at Aspåskjølen, so we retire to the car and drive down to the info boards by the Red Cross cabin and stay there with the engine idling and the heater at maximum power. While we're there, we see a new blue-white flash over Finnsåhøgda south.

The following day - Friday - we take the skis and go to Lake Hersjøen. Fantastic weather, and amazingly beautiful scenery. No wonder this is a popular cabin area.

At twilight, around nine o'clock, we put on our outfits for the evening: Coveralls... As the two evenings before, we first drive to Aspåskjølen, then south in the valley. Right after we pass Jenshaugen, we see a "star" appear over Morkavollhøgda, but "the star" moves, so then it must be a plane?

Again there is no blinking lights, and it also seems to pass strangely low in the terrain. We stop, reach for the mobile phone and record with the camera. The light is constant, yellow-white, but not brilliant. We turn off the engine to hear if there is any sound, if possible - but hear nothing. The terrain is fairly flat in this area, with no reference points, so it becomes difficult to estimate the distance to the light and its size, but we get the feeling that it's relatively close. Unfortunately a car is coming, so we have to start the engine and drive aside. The moment the car lights come on, the light "extinguishes" in the same way as we've seen before; as a light bulb that burns out. I had great expectations for the movie I took with the phone, but back at the cabin I'm disappointed; - The film shows a tiny light dot, and barely that ...

The next day, Saturday, we go skiing to lake Øyungen. It's a tiring ride on slippery skis, but the view in there is worth the effort.

At dusk, as we're ready to dress and go out, we become aware of a light through the cabin window. It reminds us of the same kind of light we've seen two evenings in a row. I open the window, take out the cellphone and start filming. The light is yellow-white, runs in a steady path over Hegsethøgda hill, sloping over the Hessdalen Valley, and towards the mountains on the east side of the valley. The light disappears before it reaches the horizon of the mountain, and just as we've seen before - it just dimmes.

This time, however, we register some kind of undulating motion in the last few seconds before it disappears. It has all the time while we have seen it had a completely straight and smooth path, but the last few seconds before it disappears, it "waves" up and down. Hege says, "Is it just me, or is it going up and down now?". So we both see the same thing. To me it seems that the light passes just above the top of mount Stordalshøgda. Before it disappears, I think the terrain below is illuminated. Although this happens at dusk and there is still some daylight, the video shows little or nothing. One can only glimpse a light dot that move on the film if you turn on the brightness and contrast at almost max.

Undulating motion! I have read a lot about this, and wave movements - or "undulating motion / oscillating flight" are something that goes way back in time in both norwegian and international UFO reports. In fact, ever since Kenneth Arnold's observation June 24, 1947, when pilot Arnold claimed to have seen nine saucer-shaped crafts in formation, moving like "saucers would bounce on the water if you throw them". With this, the term "flying saucers" was born and the modern UFO phenomenon initiated.

The undulating motion removes the last residue of doubt for me; This is actually UFOs! - and even though I've read page up and down about this - or maybe just because of that - it feels unreal to see it with my own eyes.

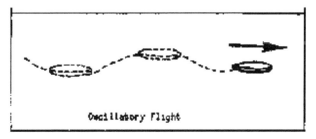

Undulating motion. From "The UFO evidence" - R. Hall.

This one evening it's a full moon. The moonlight forms a magical atmosphere, and it has become even colder. In the same way as the previous evenings, we first drive to Aspåskjølen and stand outside as long as possible without freezing our fingers and toes off, then we drive south to the parking lot at Fjellheim. At the same moment as I let go of the handbrake at Fjellheim, a light appears in the west, direction lake Øyongen.

Again, we first think of a star, then plane, but quickly see that this is the same type of light we have seen three times before. It seems to be close and in very low altitude. We turn off the engine and leave the car. I try to take a picture with the phone while Hege films. When the light passes in front of us, it extinguishes the same way as before, - but this time we seem to be able to register that it somehow flashes a little before it goes out. The flash seems to appear behind the yellow-white light point, and the color of this flash seems to be slightly reddish. We stay a little to see if it might come back, but nothing happens. It is minus 21 degrees, so it's totally ok to restart both the car, heater and blood circulation again.

What exactly is this light? Does it belong to category two as described on the information boards up on Hessdalskjølen;

> *"A yellow light moving from place to place, which can last from a few minutes to a couple of hours - the shape is often round or elliptical".*

Or is this light just a part of something bigger, - a craft? The sight of the phenomenon in which it disappeared gave me the feeling of the latter; it was almost as if one could sense the back part of a hull illuminated as it flashed. One could sense something brown or gray there ... If we saw this up close - would we then see that the round, yellow-white light was attached (in front?) of an object? Or if we saw it during the day, would we see a metallic craft?

Later in the evening, driving down from Aspåskjølen, Hege once again sees something that puts a real strain on her. We sit and talk about the big light she saw on Thursday night in front of Mount Finnsåhøgda, when she suddenly shouts THERE and points obliquely behind her. I brake and throw my head around - just in time to see a big light just above Aspåskjølen. About the same place we left just minutes ago ... Hege says the color is light green, while for me, who sees it for just one second, it looks yellow. Hege also sees a kind of curled "dash" behind the light. She thinks that the light went down into the forest - as if it lands - or crashes rather. I take a U-turn and we drive up to Aspåskjølen again. The light must have been exactly in the area where we were parked minutes ago. We joke, a little nervous, that our parking lot might be "taken"?

I must admit that I have high pulse when we drive through the forest up to the plateau. However, we cannot see either light, tracks or marks of any kind.

We go back to the cabin. It's somewhat unpleasant to think that this very big light - apparently - went to the ground, "land" or whatever? - at about the same place as we stood parked just some minutes ago.

--

The next day, it's time to pack and go home. We're talking about walking around in the area up on Aspåskjølen to find tracks - if possible - but decide not to. The snow is deep, and we have a long drive ahead of us ...

What strikes us after these evenings in Hessdalen is that the "activity" is so great. We did not expect that at all, based on the limited number of observation reports per year. This is almost like the 80's! Jon Arvid must obviously be wrong when he says that "it" is gone, so to speak? Why don't people travel to Aspåskjølen to see? It should have been both more people like ourselves here, as well as journalists and researchers from all corners of the world... At least the light that passed over Vårhuskjølen Thursday, and the light over Hegseth, across Hessdalen Friday, should be well visible to the population in the valley itself. - If they looked out the window at the appropriate times?

Before we leave, we speak to cabin owner, Geir. He asks if we've seen something, and we tell him. He himself has seen it only twice, he says... It feels almost embarrassing to say that we saw something every single night, yes, even several times a night, - so we tune it down a bit and omit most of the details.

On our way home we convince each other that it has to be because we stay outdoors that much that we actually get to see a lot. Others would probably have seen just as much - if they were out looking for it ...

6 "YOU WON'T SEE ANYTHING, ANYWAY!"

Thursday 19.04. we set course for Hessdalen again. All of my time off is already spent, so this time it has to be unpaid vacation. Useless to try something else, for what should I possibly state as a reason? "UFO-hunting" hardly falls under the "other" category that grants the right to paid vacation in the municipal sector.

The cabin is rented for three days, so now we only hope that the weather will be alright. The weather forecast threatens both with dense cloud cover, snow and strong winds, but expectations are just as great when we drive up through the curves in Hessdalslia Hillside, and it almost feels like coming home when we pass the Red Cross cabin and can view the sight inwards the valley. At the cabin, the key is in the door, and smoke is coming up the chimney. Geir has actually been here and lit up for us! How nice of him! We intend to make it easy with dinner; grilled hot dogs in bread with ketchup. Gordon Ramsay would probably have backed out, but directly from work after hours in the car it's perfect.

During the grilling, Jon Arvid stops by. After refusing a burned wiener sausage, he can tell about an observation last Sunday. A family was driving through Hessdalen and saw a light over mount

Finnsåhøgda. The light disappeared behind the mountain occasionally, but appeared again. It also appeared that the light "followed" them in the direction they were driving.

- Unfortunately for them, says Jon Arvid, I know what they've seen. It's a bright planet that appears over mount Finnsåhøgda just after sunset. It pops up every night...

We tell a little about some of our observations from the Easter. Hege, about the green light that went straight down into the forest, and I tell him about the yellow-white lights that had a straight path across the valley. That we first thought it was a star, and then planes, but that there was no sound, and that the lights just disappeared in loose air.

- Were they high up in the sky these lights you saw, asked Jon Arvid. Could it have been satellites that go so high that the sun shines on them? - No, we protested. They seemed to pass quite low in the terrain, - the last time we saw it inside Fjellheim it couldn't be many meters above the treetops...!

It's clear that Jon Arvid is a bit skeptical, but he has both seen and experienced so much that he lets it be with that. He says he won't disturb us anymore, with a grin, because we're probably going to look for UFOs? He wishes us good luck - and say we must drop by one of the days...

About half past nine, we turn off the road to the left towards Aspåskjølen, a little early, it has just begun to dusk a little. We park in the same place, but this time we only have regular clothes; that is, several layers of wool and windproof outer. The coveralls are left in boot in the back of the car for later...

A little further down the road there's a guy we see. He comes towards us, and it is our old "friend" - the farmer from the first farm below Aspåskjølen. "Do you need help?" he asks. Nope. We just want to park here and walk a little up the road and look a bit, we say. "You won't see anything anyway!" He says, spins on his heel and marches.

According to the weather forecast, it's supposed to be light weather with partly clear skies this Thursday evening. In practice, it is almost completely cloudy, - only small spots with blue sky here and there. Besides, it's more wind than notified. Immediately afterwards it starts to rain. Since it hasn't become dark yet, we decide to drive south. When we come to Vårhus, we see a strong light over Finnsåhøgda. Quite correct; here's the planet Jon Arvid talked about. Google tells us that it is Venus that is currently in the northwest after sunset.

As we drive, it appears like Venus follows parallel to the car - we know it looks like that with objects that are far away; an illusion that has probably led to countless UFO reports, - as last Sunday.

In the Easter it was meter-high snow edges on both sides of the road, and snow and ice covered the road. Now the snow edges are greatly reduced, and the road is bar. Asphalt is the first piece of road to the church, then gravel road the rest to the parking lot at Fjellheim.

Though, - to call it gravel would be an understatement... Mud is closer to the truth. It's difficult to know if you're on the road or in the field next to it. Strictly speaking, it doesn't matter. There's heavy snow melting, washboard road and hard frost heave, so better drive nicely.

At Fjellheim there are only a few cars parked this evening. It seems to be intermediate season for the cottage owners as well. We stay for half an hour. The cloud cover is dense, but in the south it has cracked up a little. A few red flashes cause the pulse to rise slightly, but the flight radar 24 app on my phone lowers it quickly to normal again; it turns out to be the evening flight from Amsterdam with course for Værnes airport.

Afterwards we drive forward in the valley again, and try to observe a little from the car in the rain. It's nothing to see; no stars, no planes, no satellites - and no flashes or other lights. After half an hour we give up, go to the cabin and go to bed. 1-0 to the farmer.

The next day we wake up to sunshine and blue sky. After a hearty portion of oatmeal for breakfast, we decide to use our skis one last time into Lake Øyongen. Jon Arvid, however, had warned us; he had experienced that it was pretty hopeless with snow scooter earlier this week, but we still have a little hope that it'll be possible to go on skis in the snowmobile tracks, where the snow has to be most compact.

It proves to be correct. It's quite ok where there are fresh scooter tracks. Outside the tracks, however, the snow is slushy. After half an hour, we come to the end of the scooter tracks. Hege makes a brave attempt, but immediately drops down with slushy snow to far up her stomach. Good thing she hit out with her hands! Otherwise, I would probably have to dug her out with a shovel...

The afternoon we spend in the sunshine outside the cabin. Clear sky, and stinging sun, it's almost as we can see the snow melt.

Around six o'clock, however, we noticed a change in the weather. Suddenly, it has become 7-8 degrees colder, raindrops and quite unpleasant abrupt. Cottage owner Geir is coming down to visit us. He asks if we're ok and whether we have what we need. We can confirm that - the only thing we are lacking is wood for the fireplace. It was cold in the Easter holidays, so now it's pretty slender inside the woodshed, but just enough for us this
weekend.

Geir asks us whether we can be interested in renting the cabin on a yearly basis. The family plans to do some maintenance. Among other things, they have talked about replacing the roof, as well as insulating. Then the cabin will keep the heat better. Of course we're interested. It's exactly something like this we've talked about and wished for!

In the evening we set the course for Aspåskjølen. Expectations are moderately optimistic. No observations yesterday, but we start with blank sheets today. The farmer is not to be seen when we park and stroll the last hundred meters up on the plateau. The weather isn't good with rain clouds hanging heavily around the mountain peaks. Fog is thick and visibility is poor. After half an hour we return to the car and drive to Hegseth. From the parking lot at the top of the road, above the cabins there, we have a view towards Hegsethhøgda Ridge to the left, Vårhuskjølen to the right, Mount Finnsåhøgda and Mount Fjellbekkhøgda in the background. At the same time, you can see both back in the valley to the south, and forward in the valley to the north. Here we can observe from the car, with the heater at full power, which is nice when the weather is so bad. However, there's nothing to observe. Neither stars, planes nor "other" lights are to be seen in the hour we sit there. We drive into Fjellheim on the piece that remains of the road, but without a counting result.

Saturday we wake to the sound of wind whistling around the corners of the cabin. A visit to the outhouse turns out to be a relatively fresh experience, and we notice that there is a little lack of isolation inside the cabin as well.

The next morning we can't conceal that we are a bit disappointed. We had great expectations after everything we saw in the Easter holidays; First and foremost, I wanted to see the light with steady path across the valley once more - and most preferably get closer to it. The weather has so far been quite miserable in the evenings. Cloudy, rain, fog and poor visibility. During the Easter holidays, where we saw "something" every single night, it was completely starlit. Could it be that the activity takes place above the cloud cover, and that's why we didn't see anything now?

No, several of the lights we saw the last time were definitely under the cloud cover. We should have exactly the same opportunities to see something similar now?

Jon Arvid mentioned that one discussed whether there was more of "it" when the moon was up. At Easter it was full moon ... But, - the moon's distance to the earth is the same regardless of the moon phase, and therefore does not affect the Earth's magnetic field, for example...

Bjørn Lillevold, son of Bjarne with the same surname, was one of Hessdalens residents who was interviewed when NRK's "Norway today" visited Hessdalen this winter. He mentioned in the program that the phenomenon might be a kind of remote controlled, unmanned "drones" sent from somewhere "outside".

- That's something similar to what the Italian Teodorani wrote and published articles about in the early 2000s. The same Teodorani mentioned the possibility of "camouflage" in a couple of his publications. In this connection, we remember what Jon Arvid mentioned; - that "they" try to camouflage themselves, like stars and planes, etc. It makes sense; if it's cloud cover, it destroys the possibility of credible camouflage... for it wouldn't necessarily benefit to imitate a star *under* the cloud cover...

These hypothetical, programmed robot drones... - what if we assume that they are only *partially* intelligent, and *partly* autonomous - what if, for example, the camouflage program is deficient? Or that the program sometimes fails?

Teodorani was on to that; you see lights that "almost" look like airplanes, but not quite... Lights that "almost" look like stars, but which can be revealed if you look carefully ... Is it so that the camouflage is imperfect and just working on the surface?

At Easter it could almost seem like it paid off to be moving. Twice we saw lights when we drove into the parking lot at Fjellheim. The same thing happened when we arrived at Aspåskjølen. Conversely, we saw nothing when we stayed in the same place for an hour or more. Patience doesn't seem to pay off...

Leif Havik mentioned similar experiences in his book;

> *"In three cases - where I have consciously noticed - the light phenomenon has suddenly appeared when I "accidentally" went out of the tent in a necessary errand. If I stood for several hours to observe, it was often impossible to detect anything at all. 90% of my 25-30 observations have occurred, either by stopping the car and going out, or by leaving the tent, house, caravan or other. It turned up right there, right THEN! That these coincidences happen once, I can understand, but when it happens on repeated occasions, with several people, likelihood of chance reduces. I definitely think that a psycic link could have happened, as I happened to travel up to Hessdalen to arbitrarily chosen times. I got to see the "same" light phenomenon in the same spot the moment the car engine was*

> *stopped, and the moment I left the car, four times! By three of the cases it was with other randomly selected comrades. Pop! ... there "it" was!"*

I haven't given particular attention to Havik's considerations in this area before. I've, in some ways, dismissed it as coincidences, and relatively irrelevant information, however, now, when I've experienced similar cases on my own, I see it in a different light...

The weather forecast reports stiff breeze throughout the day, so there will be a lot of sitting inside the cabin, just waiting. We drive a trip down to Ålen, buy supplies, and later on In the afternoon we go for a walk along the road in the Grøtådalen Valley, a side valley in the south of Hessdalen.

At dusk we're back in place at Aspåskjølen. The farmer is absent in the bad weather. Perhaps it's a little less windy, but still there's good strength in the casts. The clouds keep a sharp speed over the sky we see, with some glowing of blue sky occasionally, but just like the evenings before there is little or nothing to see. Around midnight we give up and go back to the cabin.

The next day, we stop by Jon Arvids place before heading home.

- Did you see anything?
- No, nothing, unfortunately - bad weather and visibility...

A relief to get that said, so Jon Arvid shouldn't think we're overstrained, uncritical people that see "UFOs" everywhere - which in reality is just misinterpretations of stars, planets, planes, satellites etc.

We say bye for now, start the car and leave Hessdalen for this time.

7 THE MORE SOURCES, THE MORE RELIABLE DATA

A few days after we got home, we received a sad message. Ruth Mary Moe has passed away. On the facebook page of Project Hessdalen a memoir is written:

> "It is with deep sadness we received the message that Ruth Mary Moe died Sunday, April 22, 2018, aged 76. Ruth Mary has meant a lot to the UFO case in Hessdalen. She was fearless, and dared to tell her stories. She has been a very important contributor to the UFO events in Hessdalen being known ... ... far outside Hessdalen, - far outside Trøndelag, - far beyond Norway's borders. Her stories are one of the reasons why Project Hessdalen was established."

The story she told the most, and which is probably best known from books and documentaries, is probably about the time she was working with timber together with her husband, Åge, in the early 80s. Åge was supposed to pick up a new load of timber, and meanwhile Ruth Mary was supposed to roll the logs from the previous load at place. She did so, and afterwards she sat down on the logs and lit a cigarette. As she sat there in the moonlight she became aware of a light coming from the south. It got closer, and eventually passed between her and some trees next to a cabin - she was able to estimate the distance to less than 150 meters. She compared the vehicle with a piece of bread - flat under and over - with two lights in front. As for the size, Ruth Mary said that the school bus in Hessdalen would become small in comparison ... Ruth Mary comments further that "150 meters is quite close - at least when you don't know what you're close ..."

- True! Ruth Mary's house was located on Hegseth, a short distance from the cabin we're renting. Many times when we have passed by, we have thought that we should have talked to her and heard her tell about her experiences. Now it's too late...

Hege packed everything ready, so when finished at work on Friday, all for me to do is to change clothes, fetch my backpack and get in the car and go. I filled up the tank on the mitsubishi yesterday ready. There's no time to lose! However, we had to stop by the electronics store... The last few days I read product reviews and tests on various video cameras. Especially the number of lux I'm concerned about; ie how well the camera works in low light. I have the memory from Easter still fresh. Filming or taking a picture with the camera on the mobile phone turned out to be completely wasted.

We buy a camera that'll be ok for night filming, and which has relatively heavy zoom. Now we should be well "armed" for the type of hunting we've been dreaming of!

We planned one stop. In the newspaper, we saw an advertisement for sale on the military stock by a camp we pass, and such a chance we couldn't let go. We talked a lot about lying camping on the Hessdalen mountains for the summer, but before we can do that we need a little equipment. We buy, among many other things, two good sleeping bags, proper mountain shoes, NATO sweaters and field trousers plus some other things. Now we just need an useable primus, and we're ready for the mountains. However, this will have to wait until summer. It's still only 4th May. When we arrive at Hessdalen, we saw there's a lot more snow than we thought. The road from Vårhus, through Båttjønndalen, and into lake Øyongen, we immediately see that it's impossible to drive. The same applies to the toll roads from the parking lot at Fjellheim south in the valley. It will take several weeks for these to be executable. We'll have to stick to the main road this weekend as well. It is at least dry and nice, unlike fourteen days ago.

All the snow around the cabin is gone at least, and it has dried up and started to turn green. Hege has brought a jar of flowers and puts it on the stairs. The cabin feels a little more like "ours" now, and even more so it becomes when we get some garden furniture here that we have brought from home.

It's evident that we're entering brighter times. First at half past ten it's half-dark, - we are only in May, and it's darker than dusky. Besides, the moon is shining. From Aspåskjølen we see a small flash far inside Båttjønndalen, direction Lake Øyongen. That's it. It's mostly cloud cover all over, with some blue skies in between.

The next day we wanted a better view. We park on Hessdalskjølen and start climbing the steep slopes at the foot of Mount Rogne. There is considerably more snow than it seemed from the road - it turns out - and we must almost walk in zigzag pattern upwards between the snow. We quickly learn that the newly acquired military shoes are not completely waterproof. In any case, not until they are impregnated.

Further up in the mountainside it's bare. It's almost always windy, and the snow hardly settles mid-winter. We pass several tracks for camp sites. A science Camp is held annually by the Østfold University College, and one of the bases usually resides on Rogne. Tent plugs drilled into the rock testify to challenging weather conditions during those weeks in September.

Mount Rogne is a plateau, and it's almost flat on top. The peak is at 917 meters above sea level. Here there are views in all directions; down the Gauldalen Valley to the north, down in the center of Ålen to the east, and inwards towards Hessdalen and the other mountains in the south and west.

It was at mount Rogne, Eli Bendås allegedly observed an elongated luminous phenomenon, much like a pistol bullet with the tip down - and a short-grown creature, with long arms came out of. The creature moved with some strange, jumping movements around the vessel.

It's easy to dismiss this story as nonsense, - bluff, lie, imagination or hallucinations, - had it not been for some details in the lady's descriptions, which indicate that it becomes too easy to write it off as fiction, - her descriptions fall along with similar descriptions reported by other witnesses elsewhere and at other times.

The lady described a red light in the front, and yellow-white lights at the rear. This light composition has been reported repeatedly in Hessdalen; for example, by Martin Aspås:

> *"One third of the craft is illuminated in the front, the middle is dark and the rear end is lit. It has a pulsating light in the middle of it, or it has a red light in the front and a limited, simple light behind it."*

The same is described numerous times internationally. The shape is often described as oblong, cigar or cylindrical, sometimes blunt, or rounded at one end so that it appears shaped like a pistol bullet, orlike a projectile. The red light can blink or be constant, it can be in front of OR back, or even in front of AND back (source: http://www.hyper.net/ufo-old.html).

Bendås further described that when the object went in for landing, the craft turned vertically, so that the red light pointed up. Conversely, when the object rose, the vehicle flattened so that the red light was again in front, with the yellow-white lights behind.

Exactly the same is described in other cases in Hessdalen; Martin Aspås, again:

> *"Several times we have seen an oblong object with a red light in the front. But when the object appears to land, the red light points up, and is in front when they pass in horizontal position."*

Arne Wisth, author of the book "The UFO mystery in Hessdalen", described the same when he observed a bullet-shaped craft land inside Båttjønndalen. The object turned vertically, and lowered itself to the ground. Rose, and then flattened out in a horizontal position. Furthermore, one can see the simular observation between Hjørdis Hokstad and her observation at Lånke, near Værnes airport, July 1981, - by many considered as a kind of introduction to the UFO flap in Trøndelag:

> *"Hjørdis sat at the kitchen window an early morning when she became aware that something flashed on the other side of the meadow. She took the binoculars, and the first thing she became aware of was a little "man" in gray-brown full cover. He seemed to be carrying something, and she noticed that the arms seemed unnaturally long in relation to the body. The man walked in a strange way, almost reminiscent of how the astronauts went on the moon. In the binoculars she could see that the man was moving towards an object the size of a small car. It was shaped like a pistol bullet, with the tip down. The little man went in through an opening in the object, and Hjørdis saw him no more. The object began to move, - first slowly, then it spiraled and accelerated north-east." (Havik, 87).*

Pistol ball with tip down, small "man" with long arms, moves strangely with jumping movements... In other words; now we have two almost identical stories from two older
ladies!

As a student, I learned the importance of using more data sources, and more informants.

The error most UFO skeptics do - in my opinion - is that they see each observation and data source in isolation, and overlook the fact that several sources / observations / informants together strengthen each other, and thus the reliability.

An example in this respect: If you hit heads and tails 100 times, - is there a 50% chance of getting heads 100 times in a row since each throw has a 50% chance of heads?

No! Chances are: $(1/2)^{100}$ or $1/2 \times 1/2 \times 1/2$ .... one hundred

times or 1/1267650600228229401496703205376 =
0.0000000000000000000000000007889%
chance.

You can't see each throw in isolation! Neither data sources nor UFO reports.

The larger the range, the more reliable the data. For example, if you want to make a poll, you need to ask more than one person. The more you ask (more informants / observations / sources) the more reliable the data.

So when Arne Wisth, Jon Aspås, Eli Bendås and Hjørdis Hogstad tell stories with complementing details, I find it is well worth listening to! Details in their observations are also easily recognizable in international reports.

Beyond this; Jon Arvid told us that they were a crowd of people that went up on Mount Rogne in the spring, had radio connection with Bendås so they found the landing tracks, and then noticed that all the vegetation was gone, - as if the ground in the footprints had become sterile. Bendås has passed away, but the story lives on…

In addition, several landings have been reported on Rogne, mentioned in Haviks book.

Anyway, it's extremely windy up here. We thought we were dressed well. With wool and windproof clothing, - we could still feel it right through. We have to go far down the mountainside before the wind diminishes sufficiently that we were tempted with a cup of coffee.

Back at the cabin and throughout the afternoon, Hege feels a bit under the weather. Sore throat and fever. I'm not tip top myself either. It's probably the price we paid for today's windy trip. Since it was cloudy, raining and fog tendencies, we decide to stay at the cabin this evening.

In connection with a necessary errand outside, however, I see a light that followed a straight path between the clouds in a small area of clear sky. It disappears fast, just as we observed in the Easter. However, this light seems to be quite high in the sky, so it is impossible to draw any conclusion... Iridium satellite?

Next day, we signed a contract with Geir, so now the cabin is "ours". However, it'll be a few weeks before we have the opportunity to return. Domestic commitments, confirmation weekend and so on and so forth... But in June we are aiming for a hike, and finally getting to use that tent!

8 LIGHT JUNI NIGHTS

Last weekend in June I started my vacation. Around six o'clock we arrive at the cabin. We set aside some of our equipment, repack and drive down Båttjønndalsveien Road near Vårhus. In a small shed where you can pay tolls, there is a large painting of the landscape inside Båttjønndalen Valley. In the sky over this landscape - with fishing lakes and wildlife - a flying saucer...

It's steep down to the river. A small bridge leads us over River Hesja, before we drive up the winding road on the opposite side. In first gear we move slowly upwards the many curves. Finally, we're up on Vårhuskjølen, the road goes down again, in the Finnsådalen Valley - then - once more - up some hills again - until we're in Båttjønndalen.

Here the landscape opens up; - and what a view! To the west of us we have 1000-meter peaks in a row; Mount Finnsåhøgda, Fjellbekkhøgda and Båttjønnhøgda. We drive past one fishing lake after another. The landscape from the painting down the main road becomes reality - minus the flying saucer.

The terrain is beautiful, where red-painted cottages with peat roofs are everywhere, with heifers let out on summer pastures, and where sheep with lambs lie in the roadside and taking life easy in the evening sun.

We follow the road almost to Lake Øyongen, find us a suitable tent area down by Lake Holtålstjønna, light a bonfire and start to fish. The view is impeccable with Mount Båttjønnhøgda right in front of us. The only thing that destroys the idyll is a million bugs. Thank goodness for the mosquito hats with nets we bought with us!

The next day we wake up to sunshine and take our time with the bonfire. We should probably have done better research regarding to the tent site. Sleeping on rock, even though it's covered with moss, is a hard surface for one who is passed 40, and who is occasionally afflicted with a troublesome back and neck. Hege has not slept that much either, but the coffee and the landscape immediately gets us in a better mood.

After breaking the camp we drive the rest of the road to the end. We then come down to the northwestern end of the Øyongen lake. It strikes us how incredibly large and open the whole area is. Lake Øyongen itself is 5 km long in the airline, but with bays and otters all over. It would probably take days to go around it. On all sides there are high mountains.

At the end of the road, we look straight at the mountain Rødhovde (1088 meters above sea level). In Wisth's book there is a picture of this mountain with the subtitle; "In UFO circles, it is believed that in the area behind the peak, most UFOs are registered in all parts of the district. I even got to experience one of them at a distance of three to four hundred meters just below the top":

> *"A "star" came towards us from the sky. It came towards us at a crazy speed, constantly down towards us. Now it was almost down to the mountain. Would it knock us down? Suddenly it stopped in its wild speed, just above the edge of Rødhovde. It slid slightly down to the right and somehow stood and pulsated. It has seen us! Was the first thing that struck me. How big it was, about a quarter of the moon surface. And all the colors! It changed in green, yellow, red and blue. My heart pounded in my chest, and I thought: Now we finally get time to take lots of pictures, close-ups. Then "it" was gone. "It turned off the light". "It pulled the curtains". Our comments were many and partly succulent in the next few minutes. Surprised and paralyzed, we stood there and looked around in hope that "it" would reappear."*

After buying more supplies, we find a new tent site at the opposite end of Lake Øyongen, direction southeast. Cabins are everywhere, and it is clear that this is a popular area for recreation, especially for people with money, it seems. We take our backpacks, cross some mires and find ourselves an undisturbed place in a bay well outside the cabin areas. Here is fine!

We light bonfires, and it's so windy that it's almost no bugs around. However, no luck with the fish. Lake Øyongen is probably more of a boat water, big as it is. Probably it is useless to throw from land as we do. But, hot dogs tastes good too!

The sky is nearly cloudless, full moon, but bright as in the middle of the day. After Hege crawled into the tent to sleep, I am sitting by the fire and listen to the silence as I think of a section in Haviks book;

> *"Early in the period after 1981, some people that stayed at Øyongen heard sounds that reminded of trains that passed in a tunnel just below where they stood. They could apparently follow the "train" from one end to the other, as if something passed under the ground where they were. They were scared and left. Later, it is mostly bangs and thunder that have been heard. As of today, no-one has found an explanation of the sounds."*

From the United States, we all know of rumors of so-called DUMPs;

deep underground military bases, - where things are said to happen. Such bases, according to insiders and so-called "whistle blowers", are said to be linked by a network of tunnels...

- The next day we wake up to a blue sky and 20 degrees. Perfect weather! We have planned to go up to Mount Skarvan, to the brand new research station - The Hessdalen Observatory - Norway's most highly situated research station - 1000 meters above sea level. The station is built by Project Hessdalen / Østfold University using a larger amount of money donated by norwegian multimillionaire Olav Thon; - The purpose and motivation of Thon is supposed to be "kill all conspiracy theories about UFO once and for all". What (if anything) they find remains? Thon may be surprised, I think ...

We follow the pathway up, and at the top it's not difficult to understand why mount Skarvan was chosen as a location for a new measuring station in the area . It's an absolutely stunning view in every direction. Here you get the feeling of seeing all the way to Sweden! The station, which is thought to be manned part time (as opposed to the old, automatic measuring station, Blue Box in Vårhus) is of course locked and closed, and according to a newspaper article on the web it's uncertain when the station is put into operation. It would have been extremely interesting to see what is inside of technical equipment. Considering how much money that has been injected into the project, I would think it wouldn't be small.

It's windy, but not that bad that we can sit in T-shirts at the top, drink coffee and have lunch.

In the evening we drive into Båttjønndalen Valley again in search of a current tent site. Next to Lake Båttjønna itself, we find our little "paradise". Good access to crusty birch wood for the bonfire, and flat, soft surface for the tent.

Our camp.

We are right at the foot of mount Fjellbekkhøgda / Finnsåhøgda, and look straight up in the passage between the peaks. In other words, we are now right at the center for the activity from the 80s. I have no digests on how many UFO reports I've read where an object is described as having taken the course into this gap between the mountains and disappeared out of sight (seen from Aspåskjølen).

Often the aforementioned oblong object of yellow and red light, often described as cigar shaped, like a projectile, or as an egg cut in half. As the objects often passed from south to north in this area - along the Båttjøndalen Valley - the mountains in the west became a perfect observation point.

Both Fjellbekkhøgda and Finnsåhøgda were used as observation posts during the field actions in the 80s, and several of the photos that are on the Project Hessdalen website are taken from here.

One of those who took the most (and best) pictures of the phenomenon was Arne P. Thomassen from Arendal. Thomassen managed to document the aforementioned undulating motion; The image shows an object in a undulating motion from left to right - recorded by using long exposure time, - approx. 30 seconds. - Just the same as we had seen in the Easter.

Leif Havik had apparently an experience in the area behind mount Fjellbekhøgda in 1983:

> *"...he saw a shiny-silver object that slowly slipped out of an invisible portal in the sky. The distance was impossible to calculate, but it was "close enough" to see the details of the hull. It looked like a fuselage without wings, and it was clearly composed of plates. Although it was gleaming in silver color, there were parts that were like soot-colored glass, especially below in the front. The entire hull eventually appeared and it stopped. Throughout this phase, Leif felt a tingling sensation in his arms and legs and a pressure in his head. It was an unpleasant feeling, and it was as if "something" deprived Leif of his will. Something reasonably told him that he should flee from there while something else "locked" him to the bog where he was sitting. Leif felt an intense high frequency beeping inside his head, and there was an unpleasant pressure on his forehead.*
>
> *Leif explains further: "A faintly reflective shine, possibly light, was fluttering along the side of the hull. It was a kind of nondescript, woolly coating, most reminiscent of light, or rather illuminated smoke. Suddenly it felt as if my head would burst, and there was an indescribable pain in my forehead. Then I don't really know what happened. The next thing I remember was that I sat looking over the rocky landscape wondering that it had become so dark. Now there was no pain in the head, and the wingless fuselage was gone. I had to sort my mind and leaned against the stone and rolled a cigarette. Then it was as if a cassette player started, and an authoritative and clear voice began to speak. One lesson was read after another. After a while, the "cassette player" stopped. I suddenly felt that I wanted to go home. I put my back pack on, and I quickly made my way back up to the car." (Source: hessdalen.org)*

- Understandable...

According to Jon Arvid, Erling Strand also had a daylight observation behind Mount Finnsåhøgda. Jon Arvid said it this way:

> *"He (Erling Strand) saw the same thing that I saw. But he says he can't talk about it publicly!"*

However, I read about this in an interview with Strand. To the website "unexplained mysteries" he states the following:

> *- Even if I had several daytime observations, where I have seen flying discs etc., I cannot say where these come from. Many say they have to come from exo planets. How do they know? Why not another time, another dimension or maybe even more far-fetched. Even if I have had daytime observations, and know such exists, I do not connect to the HP. It may be completely different things.*

So Strand speaks partly about it publicly, but is for the time being reticent to Norwegian media. However, during the interview with NRK's "Norway today" from this winter, he went so far as to say that "I have seen similar things myself", - implicitly: craft / vehicle - but I do not draw *that* conclusion, - implied: That it's "visitors".

I share Strand's attitude regarding drawing conclusions from an overly thin data base. But it is allowed to speculate …

It's difficult to sleep this night. First, it's too cold, even with woolen sweaters and leg warmers in the sleeping bag. It's June and summer, but we are at 800 meters above sea level…

But after the sun has risen, it is suddenly too hot. The tent feels like a sauna! We have to cook and drink two pots of coffee before feeling ourselves again. Afterwards we drive in to Lake Hersjøen to see if we can spot Jon Arvids cabin, but it turns out easier said than done, - There's *a lot* of cabins there …

After eating dinner, we drive an evening trip through Båttjønndalen. The plan really is to go fishing, but since it hasn't been raining for several weeks, the soil is hard as stone. I perforate the area around the cabin, but after half an hour of wear and tear I have still not dug up more than three small earthworms… Thus the fishing rods are left in the cabin.

It's midnight before we go down from Vårhuskjølen. In one of the sharpest turns we meet a car. It turns out to be Bjørn Lillevold, which we recognize from the NRK broadcast this winter. Is he looking for UFOs? At this point, the road is so narrow that I have to back a hundred meters to the nearest shoulder.

Probably he must have seen *something* , even on bright summer nights we thought - especially when he bothers to drive in here at night?

However, we are exhausted and drive down to the cabin. It's totally okay to find a mattress after three days in tent, and we sleep like babies until late in the morning the next day.

We wake up to cloudy weather and a fairly different temperature. The weather forecast reports rain and winds, and it will continue for several days ... After discussing options, we agree to go home.

--

- It has been full moon and clear weather, as in the Easter - yet we haven't seen the trace of the phenomenon. Does it HAVE to be dark? No, we've read about many observations made during summer time as well. But it's obviously harder to see a light up against a light background, versus a dark one. Maybe we are simply dependent on "luck" in the summer?

At home we watched a documentary about Hessdalen on youtube. Here, Erling Strand speaks of, among other things, radar observations in Hessdalen, - where phenomena have been invisible to the eye, but nevertheless reflected radar waves and thus been visible on the computer screen, so that one has been able to follow it through the valley from A to B.

Already in the 80's, attempts were made to photograph with infrared film in Hessdalen, and several have speculated whether the lights in Hessdalen are moving in and out of the visible area of the electromagnetic spectrum. Occasionally into the infrared range, and sometimes into the ultraviolet range, which is closest to visible light on either side of the scale. Perhaps the phenomena are far more frequent than we can see with our eyes? Perhaps it's so that the lights are often on the edge of the visible part of the electromagnetic spectrum and therefore appear to be dim and difficult to spot, especially in the bright summer months?

9 HIDE AND SEEK

The weather is brilliant as we arrive in the afternoon, - sun and blue skies and approx. 25 degrees. First, we drive into Båttjønndalen and go fishing, but the fish turns out to be a little bit tedious in the heat, and back at the cabin it's grilled burgers instead of trout.

We've come a long way out in July now, and it's getting darker in the evenings. As an observation spot this evening, we've decided to go for Slettælet, a plateau near lake Øyongen, between the mountains Skarvan and Morkavollhøgda. Here there are good views in all directions. We have brought with us folding chairs, but even though it's July and nice summer temperatures, it's notable that we're in the mountains. The wind blows right through our woolen jumpers. Two and a half hours we stay at Slettælet without seeing anything. At one AM we give up and return to the cabin. It has been a long day, and Hege falls asleep on the short drive back to the cabin.

As we turn and drive down the courtyard towards the cabin, a light appears in the southwest. I tear up the handbrake, grab the camcorder and jump out of the car in one motion. Hege wakes up. - Do you see anything? There, yes ... Oh my god!

It seems to be the same kind of light we saw several times at Easter. The light holds a steady path - across the valley. From southwest to east. The light is far south in the valley - roughly above Slettælet, apparently - where we stood parked just a few minutes ago! It's yellow-white, but relatively pale to look at. A soft, almost slightly transparent, light. I press "record". The light stops, then the brightness increases for a few seconds - suddenly - it's gone! As if a switch is turned off.

However, I messed up so much with the camera - zooming in at the wrong place, zooming out, etc. - that I'm not really studying the phenomenon in particular detail. From our position and to the light it is several kilometers. Obviously, this light must have been big!

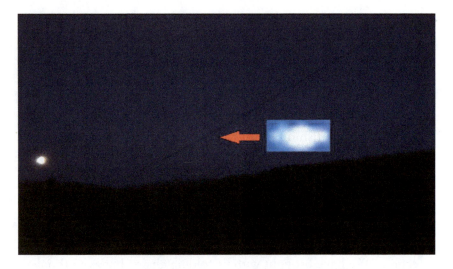

The arrow shows where it disappeared.

It's almost full moon, and not very dark. I wish I'd rather have studied the phenomenon and got a clearer observation instead of filming.

A number of questions arise: The phenomenon disappeared immediately after I started filming ... Coincidence? Did the light pass over Slettælet where we stood parked minutes ago? Would it have appeared if we were still parked up there?

"Hide and seek", I thought to myself...

At home, I transfer the footage to my laptop. I take out a series of still images - especially when it's at the brightest just before it disappears. When I magnify, and turn up contrast, it looks a lot like a "saucer"... Or as the "hat" Wisth described, "the old-fashioned gentleman's hat" Ruth Mary told about...

At the cabin, I check Flight Radar 24. Not a single flight over Trondelag last 10 minutes. Not that it is necessary to check the app - we clearly saw that this wasn't a plane. It went way too low, and considerably slower than normal flight speed. Moreover, it had no navigation lights flashing. Only a steady yellow-white light. In addition, - planes usually don't stop and disappear into thin air!

We go to bed and try to sleep. It's late at night, but getting a nap is easier said than done. It's unbearably hot inside the cabin, and we've just seen a UFO...!

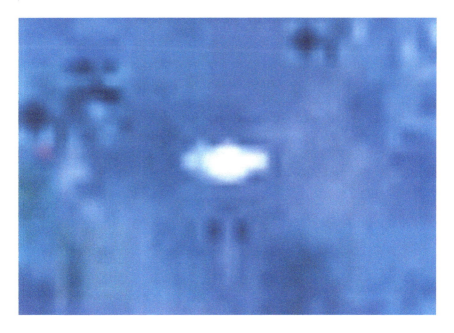

Zoomed in.

Friday we wake up to beautiful weather. The weather forecast promises sunshine, blue skies and 30 degrees during the day. We fill up the water bottles, drive the road inwards Båttjønndalen Valley and park under the foot of Finnsåhøgda. We follow the pathway up to the right of the stream that's almost dry after the hot and arid weather we've had this summer.

Mount Finnsåhøgda was used as an observation post in the early 80s, and Science Camp has had a base here during the field actions in September each year, so the pathway is easy to follow. Not long after we're up in the gap between Mount Fjellbekkhøgda and Mount Finnsåhøgda.

In the 80's, the phenomena used to pass just about here. Occasionally through the ravine, other times in the forefront, with the mountain as a backdrop. Hege says that being here gives her a very special feeling. We're now in the concentrated area with the most ufo sightings in the world through all ages...

We continue on to the top. It's windy, but we're wearing shorts and I can take off my t-shirt because of the heat. What a contrast to the coveralls we used this winter! From the top of Finnsåhøgda we have views to the mountains southwest and west of Hessdalen. Miles of miles with deserted mountain range.

On our way down, we have fantastic views over Båttjønndalen Valley with its countless small and large ponds. They are mostly reminiscent of small mirrors where they lie, reflecting the sunshine around the landscape. We take pictures right and left...

Båttjønndalen seen from Finnsåhøgda.

Many of the best known images of UFOs in the 80s are taken from here. Some of them are on the Project Hessdalen website. However, photographing light sources in the dark isn't an easy task, and the result often does not do it justice to what has been seen. In Hessdalen, long exposure time has often been used, so that the phenomenons movements have been recorded in the picture. Most are taken at a long distance and then greatly enlarged. Several of them are overexposed, unfortunately. The pictures show a powerful light source, but never what's possibly "behind" the light. By just looking at the pictures, one can easily form an erroneous impression of how the phenomena would have looked in reality.

- Back at the cabin we decide to drive in to Hersjøen, and go swimming. Several people have had the same idea - obviously - because there are people swimming from both cabin owners and Hessdalen residents of all ages around the whole of Lake Hersjøen.

It's fresh, but considering that there was snow up in the mountains until the end of June, the water temperature is not that bad.

Back at the cabin we fire up the grill and chill in the shade. Jon Arvid stops by. We tell him that we've not seen anything of significance since Easter, - UNTIL last night, and tell about the light we saw last night. We point out the direction from where we're sitting.

Jon Arvid tells us about *his* cabin. He asks if we want to see it - we could drive?

So - for the second time today we drive towards Lake Hersjøen. The cabin is sighted surprisingly high up in the hillside, and has magnificent views over Lake Hersjøen, further north, into Lake Øyongen, Mount Rødhovde, Mount Skarvan - one can even see Mount Finnsåhøgda in the distance.

We ask what Jon Arvid has seen from here, and he tells several stories I recognize from books and report collections. Jon Arvid and his cabin are mentioned in a section in Wisth's book as well:

> *"Jon Arvid Aspås always spends the summer at a cabin near lake Hersjøen along with his family. The cabin is on a hill with a good view of the valley. The sun was still up at 19.25 on September 3, 1982. The sky was clear, and Jon Arvid and the kids worked on the field. Then they saw something coming from the south in the sky. The object was like a fuselage without wings. Silver metallic, glossy in color. It was probably approx. 2 km. away from them.*
>
> *- It turned and went a bit east of us. It was so close that we could also observe it from below. We saw absolutely no wings. It reminded us most about old airships that we have seen pictures of. No sound was to be heard.*
>
> *Jon Arvid ran to get the binoculars. As he came back, "the thing" disappeared into a cloud.*
>
> *- It wasn't big. We wondered why we couldn't see it coming out of there again. But it was gone."*

One story is new to me; In the 80's, a light was observed in the middle of Hersjøen from one of the cabins. In binoculars it looked like a "boat that burned". Jon Arvid is an avid moose hunter, and recently they brought a new guy in the hunting team. It turned out that he was just a little kid when this happened, and was staying at one of the cabins on the opposite side of Lake Hersjøen. He and his family saw the same light and rowed out on the water to check. When they came out to the area where the light was, it bubbled up from the depth...

From Jon Arvids cabin you can also see inwards towards Slettælet where we stood parked yesterday. We point, and mention that we've seen "it" four times now in almost identical orbit, apparently with offspring in the area Lake Øyongen, Mount Morkavollhøgda, Skarvan, Slettælet, - southwest to the east - the fifth time, it turned and came against us while we stood in Aspåskjølen.

In the 80's it also had a kind of "regular" path, says Jon Arvid - but at that time it was usually from south to north. Often through Båttjønndalen Valley, towards, or along Mount Finnsåhøgda.

Could it be that it has "changed" the main path? On the Project Hessdalen website is an interesting article by Torbjørn Aamodt (2017). It consists of an analysis of movement - routes / courses - as described in the observation reports that are in the database of Project Hessdalen, up against geological maps from NGU - Norway's Geological Surveys - which show where different rocks are located - as well as magnetic anomalies associated to these. Aamodt writes:

> *"In the magnetic anomaly map, the light/object trajectories match impressively well with magnetic anomalies, indicating that lights/objects are moving from one anomaly to another."*

So, from the analysis, the lights/objects may appear to follow fixed routes or tracks and that these appear to be connected with magnetic fields in the area.

Some have wondered if the UFOs "charge" - or somehow extracts energy in specific areas of the Hessdalen valley. Thus Hessdalen as a type of "charging station". This theory was mentioned in the journal "UFO" already in the early 80s:

> "... the theory that they (the UFOs) flew here to" recharge "! This was justified by the fact that they came in one by one, and stood over the same place in the mountain. The area here should be highly magnetic, and there are a lot of metals and minerals in the mountains. Is there a "UFO magnetic" line through this area?"

Other theories go in the direction of phenomena that are" shuttled in and out" in specific areas linked to magnetic fields etc. Hessdalen as a kind of" portal "where the special geophysical conditions facilitate "entry / exit"? This theory was first mentioned in Trondheim newspaper Adresseavisen's debate pages, - in a reader's letter 21.12.83 (from "UFO" no. 2 1983):

> "A "philosopher" suggests in a reader's letter the 21st of december the idea that many of the electromagnetic fields in quartz deposits - which can be found in Hessdalen - can be "site" for vessels that materialize. Ie that the mountains in the valley serve as a kind of "portal" into our time and the world."

Morkavollhøgda: Quartz.

Jon Arvid is obviously more accustomed to winding gravel roads than me, and keeps good speed on the return trip. It's a large cloud of dust behind the station wagon. It hasn't been raining for several weeks and the gravel is crunchy.

We use the chance to ask again about this thing with "camouflage":

- Oh, I've seen that many times. We stood at Aspåskjølen in the 80s and looked at two moons, for example. One real and one who stood up next to the real moon and "pretended"

... Speaking of the moon. Tonight it's supposed to be a lunar eclipse. But it'll probably be below the horizon while the eclipse is on, so it's questionable if we'll be able to see anything.

Back at Hegseth Jon Arvid asks if we want a cup of coffee. Donuts are presented and we sit down in the sofa.

- You don't get tired of questions from people who want to talk about UFOs with you? - Well, sometimes, yes. But once you have been stupid enough to speak about this, you just have to keep going...

The other day he was invited at a 60th birthday gathering with many guests. Jon Arvid has been featured both in newspapers and on TV, so he's often recognized. Here, as well, and instead of people coming over one by one, he got up at the dinner table and told a little about his experiences unsolicited. In this way he escaped the same questions over and over and having to repeat the same stories.

After hearing that we'll not bother him with more UFO talk for tonight. Instead, the conversation turns into moose hunting and cloudberries. The time is half past eleven before we stroll down to the cabin.

At dusk we drive Båttjønndalen back and forth without seeing anything but a rabbit crossing the road. However, we went so high up that we see the last part of the lunar eclipse. We wondered if "they" can be influenced by this phenomenon?

Along the way, we discuss the light from yesterday. It disappeared a second after I pressed the record button. People made similar experiences in the 80s. Havik mentions a little about this in his book from 1987:

> *"How could it happen that the light phenomenon in Hessdalen just disappeared in nothing in September 1983, when Arne Thomassen shone on it with a flashlight. It disappeared in nothing when I blinked with the headlights of the car, in the fall of 1982. How could it happen that the light phenomenon in Hessdalen disappeared into nothing when trying to study it through binoculars, or attempted to take a picture of it? It was gone in "nothing" by two cases when I was taking pictures of it. It happened in Falun, Sweden, on January 9, 1985, when a man was trying to photograph a light phenomenon. The same happened countless times when a fire guard in Yakima lifted the binoculars to look at the light."*

It may be that these hypothetical "probes" Teodorani talk about, possibly are programmed to respond (disappear) to electrical impulses if a device - for example a video camera – is turned on? Or can it possibly be that a hypothetical technology can be so developed and advanced that it is capable of capturing, analyzing and interpreting electrical impulses emitted from the brain - a kind of "technical telepathy"? An exciting and frightening thought...

- Around midnight we park at Slettælet. I have a slight hope that the same type of light that last night will appear at the same time and in the same place. If so, we have ringside seats from here! However, it doesn't. After two hours we give up, drive to the cabin and go to bed.

On the trip down towards Fjellheim, Hege sees a large flash just above the mountain in front. We stop and study the horizon in front of us. Will it show up again?

Again we remember what Jon Arvid had said: That in the 80s one discussed whether there was a connection... that often - after seeing flash - it was possible to see something more - vehicles, crafts...

Teodorani has also been onto this in his articles. He discusses whether "sudden flashes everywhere in the valley" is a trigger mechanism for other types of phenomena in Hessdalen. Leif Havik's book gives an example of such a connection between flash and craft:

> *"Then came a huge grey hull. It had a large red light at each end. It came sliding slowly and quietly from the south just above the treetops, across the fields and over the water in an arc. It slowly dropped below the treetop level, and it could have been only 2-300 meters away. It disappeared beyond the water and behind the hills in the background. The observers also noticed a powerful light flash that most of all looked like photo blitz."*

Another example from Nordic UFO Newsletter no. 1 1988:

> *"A few minutes later they saw a big flash that lit up the sky against Ålen. The light had a slight greenish shade. They stopped the car and turned off the car lights after another flash. Each flash lasted 3-4 seconds, with a one-minute interval between them. Shortly after the last flash, they saw an object flying low in the terrain. The object was prism-shaped and equipped with four landing feet. All details were visible and clear. The object came down in front of the car, slowly flew forward, then made a sudden stop and then disappeared straight into the air."*

This time, however, nothing more happens after the flash.

The next day, it is time to return home, but we got time for one more trip before the summer holidays are over.

Expectations are turned slightly up now that we saw "it" again, and in August the evenings begin to darken again.

10 YOU SHOULD HAVE BEEN WITH ME

On the Project Hessdalen website, - under the tab "latest observations", we read:

Date: 29.07. 2018 Time: 23:30 Location: Lake Øyungen, Hessdalen. Observers: Jon Arvid Aspås and two more.

> *"Jon Arvid was with two others in a boat on Øyungen. While sitting in the boat, they spotted a large, bright light in the south-east, towards Lake Hersjøen. The light was just next to the moon. Jon Arvid saw first a strong flash. There were some clouds, so the light was not seen all the time. The light moved to the west. They saw it for approx. 5 minutes. Jon Arvid noted the strength and size."*

A week ago we sat in the living room with Jon Arvid and heard him tell that it was a long time since he had seen something and that he would like to see *"it"* again - and then it takes only a few days!

We also notice that Jon Arvid saw a strong flash ahead of the actual observation...

Speaking of Jon Arvid, we've long been talking about bringing a gift for him. He doesn't drink liquor, he has said, so we have to think of something other than the brandy we first thought of. After a little back and forth, we buy a big orchid as a thank for all the help, sightseeing, coffee and interesting conversations.

We drive straight into his courtyard immediately as we arrive at Hessdalen this Monday in
the last week of the holiday. The first thing Jon Arvid says is: - You should have been with me last Monday! Jon Arvid talks enthusiastically, and we get to hear details beyond what is stated in the report. - It was bigger than the moon!

Jon Arvid sat up on Mount Hersjøhøgda throughout Tuesday night, hoping that "it" would reappear. It didn't, but it tells alot when a man of his age - who has already seen the phenomenon over 100 times before - sits up on a mountain a whole night to observe. It necessarily have made an impression!

We on our side show him the pictures from our observation the previous trip to Hessdalen. Zoomed, with upgraded contrast and brightness, it resembles as previously mentioned a kind of saucer.

- Look at that... Yes, says Jon Arvid. That is just about the way they used to look like... He mentions an observation he had himself in year 2000 down in Hessdalslia on a trip to Ålen, when he saw a light in the direction of Øggdalen and Mount Litjfjellet. Through binoculars he saw that the shape was like a hat with a rim at the bottom.

Jon Arvid thanks us for the flowers. We get in the car, drive down to the cabin and start unpacking.

At dusk we are back in place at Slettælet. We park and bring out our folding chairs. Well dressed, with wool - as well as windproof - and with our sleeping bags folded over us at the top - it becomes quite comfortable to be UFO hunters this evening.

It's virtually clear sky and starlit. We see small and large flashes in several colors and directions. Among other things, a quite powerful one in the direction south between Mount Hersjøhøgda and Mount Morkavollhøgda. About five minutes past midnight, a light appears

over the top of just Morkavollhøgda. There are some irregular movements in the
beginning, but then it takes a steady path, - straight towards us!

I've already picked up the camcorder and try frantically to zoom in on the light. However, it is easier said than done, as it passes right over our heads. Quite *high* above us. Exactly how high is difficult to estimate, as it appears as a light towards an otherwise dark sky. The light disappears over mount Skarvan and out of sight.

About half an hour later, 00:36, a similar light appears. Again it shows up over Mount Morkavollhøgda, but this time it turns and disappears over Lake Øyongen in the direction of Mount Rødhovde in the north-west. Again, the camcorder is on, rolling…

Can these lights be satellites? Extremely bright satellites, if so! We have more a feeling of that both of these lights are something similar to those we saw from the parking lot at Fjellheim in the Easter. The difference is that in the Easter they came down the mountainside towards us, - increasingly closer, and ever lower - before they suddenly disappeared. This time, they seem to pass high above us.

It's two o'clock before we return to the cabin without having seen anything more of importance.

- Tuesday morning we pack our bags and set course for today's goal: Mount Morkavollhøgda. We've talked about getting up at this mountain for a long time. As I said, the lights have seemed to kind of "originate" from behind this mountain. How does it look behind the top?

We miss the pathway upwards and get a relatively hard and steep ascent. We're therefore both sweaty and weary as we arrive at the top, but the better it is to sit down and simply enjoy the view. It is formidable! From the cairn top we have a full overview of the whole great Lake Øyongen area with surrounding mountains.

Øyongen seen from the top of Morkavollhøgda.

Morkavollhøgda was the site for one of three observation bases under the so-called "triangle project" in 1997. The other two bases were located on Mount Rogne and Finnsåhøgda respectively. As the name implies: Together, the three peaks formed a triangle, and the purpose was to observe, record and photograph any phenomena that appeared inside the
triangle and in this way determine distance, direction, movements etc.

The first - and so far - *only* field action, was held October 10-12, 1997. Two spectacular observations were made, and several interesting pictures were taken. There's a site on the net that documents the events this weekend:

Summary of report 1:

> *"At 21:15 Andreas got eye on a bright light a little west of the top of Morkavollhøgda. The light source began to go up and down behind the mountain, almost like a yo-yo. The light source itself consisted of a*

pyramid-shaped surface that shone strongly. Every time the light source disappeared down behind the mountain, we observed a beam of light that lit up in the air, the light coming from the same place as the light source had gone down. This happened several times, before the light source disappeared down behind the mountain for the last time and disappeared."

Summary of report 2:

"Approx. At 23:45, Akhtar pointed out a red light west of Lake Øyongen. The light source changed color from red to yellow-white. Akhtar began taking pictures of the phenomenon. The light source moved back and forth over Øyongen, before it disappeared south and behind Morkavollhøgda so that we couldn't see it anymore.

Right after this, half of the western part of Øyongen was illuminated quite vigorously by a white light. It seemed that a huge "spotlight" was directed towards the water. The light that lit up the water was clearly delimited. We could not see the actual source, but it seemed that the spotlight came from the area behind Morkavollhøgda where the light ball had disappeared.

There is an island in the middle of lake Øyungen called Storholmen. We could not see this island in the dark, but we saw the whole island when this "floodlight" was turned on. This "spotlight" lit up the lake a few seconds at a time, before it became dark. A few minutes passed between each time the light illuminated the lake. The beam of light swept slightly over the western part of lake Øyongen, but remained quite calm. This happened a few times before the "spotlight" was turned off for good."

These are the reports I have in mind as I look out over the huge Lake Øyongen area. No wonder why the participants experienced the events as both scary and unpleasant!

Morkavollhøgda has thus allegedly been the scene of spectacular events, and both lights we saw yesterday came from the top, - just about here where we are now ... Again, - can it supposedly be extra bright satellites we saw? These - as known - can reflect sunlight before and after sunrise / sunset - if they go sufficiently high?

Back at the cabin, I download three different "satellite tracker" apps on the phone. These are based on GPS, and show potentially visible satellite passages - as well as rockets and space debris that also can reflect sunlight - within a selected radius.

In addition, I download the app "Starlight" which recognizes and identifies stars and planets through the camera lens on the phone. It's good to keep track of exactly where different planets and stars are at any given time.

- Well down from mount Morkavollhøgda we continue along Øyongen and turn left towards lake Elgsjøen. In there is a cabin that sells traditional food of the area; cheese and cured meat etc. It isn't open now, but it's very idyllic in any case. It feels like driving around in a postcard, where the sheep are lying down in the shade around the red painted cabin walls.

Inside Lake Elgsjøen, one of the probably most remarkable events in Hessdalen happened:

> *"In September 1980 a grouse hunter witnessed an event that he would probably remember throughout his life. He had entered the mountains south of the lake. There he was going to hunt with two comrades. It was brilliant weather, with clear skies and fine autumn air. It was about 11.30 in the morning when he suddenly felt something came behind him as he saw a shadow sliding in the heather. He turned, and just a few feet away from him, three magnificent objects resembling saucers hung in the air. They had an indescribably beautiful red color that sparkled in the sunlight. Around the "saucers" there was a kind of rim or carrying wing. This rim was composed of pipes similar to organ pipes, and it was spinning around. At the top of the "saucers" there was an elevation, and on the right, something like antennas. Below each of the items were two holes, one on each side. The material from which the objects were made was difficult to describe, and it was mostly reminiscent of a mixture of glass and stone. The objects were about 4 meters in diameter, and they emitted a slight buzzing sound. Suddenly, as on command, all three objects rized upright with the top facing the direction of speed. In formation they disappeared over the mountains to the north."(Havik,*

87).

It belongs to the story that the grouse hunter sold his rifle shortly after…

In connection with this observation, it's worth noting the similarities with the "hat" that Wisth described as one of the usual UFO categories in Hessdalen, and "the gentleman hat with rim "Ruth-Mary told about, as well as Jon Arvid's observation of a "hat-like" object down in Hessdalslia hill. In Wisth's book there is a photograph of the "hat" - in addition to the cover
photo which is also of the "hat" - with the caption:

> *"The hat" is a UFO model we've got many pictures of. They are 5-6 meters in diameter and turn transversely as they fly fast."*

This thing about saucers reported to turn across / rise upwards - then take off at high speed with the bottom towards the speed direction - is otherwise something that is also described
repeatedly internationally. Again, the fact that several independent sources together strengthen the reliability…

After eating dinner, we drive up to Aspåskjølen as Hege suggests. She observed spectacular things from there at Easter that was so brief that I didn't get to see it. Her hope is that I'll see something similar.

We stay at Aspåskjølen for about half an hour, but experiences like at Easter are absent. However, we see a couple of flashes far intrough the valley, and that's good news as we head for Slettælet.

We barely reach to park until another light pops up. Again, over the black silhouette of Mount Morkavollhøgda. It passes over us and disappears behind Mount Skarvan. Shortly after, a similar light appears. Again, above the top of Morkavollhøgda, the same course and direction. Both times I check the satellite apps I've downloaded. According to them there shall be no satellites within 50 km radius at the moment. Both lights appeared above the highest point on Morkavollhøgda, - exactly where we sat and ate lunch earlier today.

Satellites do not follow corridors such as airplanes... So, it's relatively strange that all four lights follow exactly the same course and path. What are the odds of that? All four lights kind of fit with how I think satellites look and behave - apart from the brightness of course - but the apps insist stubbornly that the lights are NOT satellites...

On Wednesday morning we woke to rain and grey weather. In addition, the wind howls around the cabin. The weather forecast reports wind up to 15 meters per second - and that's down in the valley! It's not very tempting to go to the mountains today...

Instead, we drive to Røros town and hope the weather will clear up and calm down towards the evening.

However, there's shallow and poor vision when we drive up to Slettælet at dusk. In order to have a bit of visibility at all, the engine must idle and the windscreen wipers go uninterrupted.

No "satellites" are to be seen tonight. However, we register a red flash.
Red flashes are unusual, we've understood. As a rule, it's either yellow, white, blue, or even more rare - green flashes that's been seen.

Red light indicates low energy, I read on wikipedia: "Red has the longest wavelength, and thus the least energy, violet is the most "energy rich "color." The spectrum goes from red (longest wavelength) via orange, yellow, green, blue, indigo and purple (shortest wavelength).

--

A little digression: American Paul R. Hill was employed as an engineer in NASA. After having observed two flying saucers himself in 1952, he began to collect and analyze data concerning UFOs but could not publish anything about the subject while he was employed by NASA / received pension. However, after Hill died in 1991, it was possible to publish the
book he finished already in the 70s; Unconventional Flying Objects - a scientific analysis. This book was released in 1995.

Hill writes:

> *"All UFO colors stem from energetic, ionizing radiation or radiations generated by the UFO which ionize the air. The energy the electron imparts to each photon determines its wavelength and color. Air molecules can radiate in a kaleidoscope of colors - any color of the spectrum. Of all the visible colors, red and orange correspond to the least energy. They are also the 2 most common colors associated with UFO low-power operation such as hovering or low-power maneuvers. The electrons have been given the ionization energy (but not much more) and cascade down in small energy drops corresponding to red or orange. This is statistically probable as there are more small drops available than big ones. Blue color requires a relatively high energy activation. Blue, white and blue-white are the most common colors of high energy maneuvers."*

Havik also writes about UFOs and colors in Hessdalen:

> *"The phenomenon can be perceived as reddish-brown, reddish-orange, yellow-white or blue light-balls. - It has often been seen that the higher the speed the phenomenon has, the whiter the light is. Stationary light balls usually have a warm yellow or reddish color."*

It's important in this context to keep in mind that Hill's book was written in the 70s, but not published until after his death, in 1995. Havik's book was published in 1987. Havik and Hill had therefore NO opportunity to read each other's books! Still, what they write is almost coincidental!

--

Tuesday morning we wake up to glorious weather. The rain and dense fog have been replaced with blue skies, sunshine and 20 degrees. Hessdalen shows us again it's very best side.

Good news, because today we've thought about a long trip. Ever since we were up at Finnsåhøgda, we've talked about getting up on the "neighbor" – Mount Fjellbekkhøgda - and seeing more of the terrain in the mountainside in the west. Perhaps we look right into

Ledalen too - where Jon Arvid, together with his brother-in-law Åge and neighbor Bjarne, saw the three egg-shaped objects during the scooter trip in 1982?

It was in addition in Ledalen that three moose hunters in the fall of 1984 found a piece of swamp, carved, lifted up and placed next to the hole it had come from. The piece - which was pentagonal, 4 x 5 meters and cut with laser precision - must have weighed a few tons. There were no traces of machinery! In addition, a 100% identical anthill - the same shape and size -
was found on Andøya in Troms two years earlier.

This happened in the 80's, but we've talked about visiting Ledalen Valley to find out what might still be left of tracks.

From the top of Mount Fjellbekkhøgda (1078 meters above sea level) we see that it will possibly be a relatively strenuous trip. It is far into Ledalen. Very far! Again: It strikes us how huge the area is. Solid mountain plateau as far as the eye can see.

At the very beginning of the UFO wave in Hessdalen - in December 1981 - it was believed that the objects went down in the area behind Finnsåhøgda and possibly landed.

From Norwegian UFO Newsletter no. 2 1982:

> *"... an object has been observed to come from the south-west, stop over Finnsåhøgda, go vertically down behind the mountain, then come up again, and then return back in about the same route to the south-west. In some cases, the object has gone up and down several times behind the mountain. The object was illuminated and shiny, like a disc, possibly a somewhat oval ball (egg-shaped) with relatively sharp contours. It can be compared to the moon when it comes to light and contours.*
>
> *Finnsåhøgda is 3 kilometers in line from the observer's position. In one case, the object sank to the forefront of the mountain so that the witnesses could see the luminous object down to the ground, not far from the lower yard, with the mountain as the backdrop. When one later went there to investigate, no visible traces were found in the snow. No sound was*

heard. Observers included Ruth-Mary Moe, Åge Moe and John Aspås. Otherwise, a large number of people have seen the object from Aspåskjølen."

By the way, Ruth-Mary said in connection with these introductory observations that "we thought this was a two-three nights happening, then it would be over - but it turned out that it wasn't going to be like that...! "

- True! It's been 37 years now...

We find shelter for the wind, sit down and pick up our lunch from the bag. Suddenly we hear a noticeable buzzing sound. It turns out to be undramatic; an overgrown bumblebee that have strayed on a mountain tour...

Buzzing sound is otherwise recurring in UFO reports, cf. the aforementioned grouse hunter, and his observation inside Lake Elgsjøen; he described the sound the three saucers gave as something like "a bumblebee stuffed in a matchbox".

In international UFO reports, it is sometimes called "humming noise". The web site "Best ufo resources" - hypernet.com/ufo/overview - is literally a lexicon for UFO facts. About sound it says:

> *" Researchers classify several groups of UFO sounds: 1/ low pitch (hum, buzz "like swarm of bees", that "can be felt, as well as heard"), 2/ high-pitch (whine, hissing, shrill whir, high pitched hum/ drill), 3/ highest pitch (shrieking, piercing whistle) or "signals" (shrill beeping, modulated whistle), 4/ rush of air (release of air, swishing, fluttering), but rarely also 5/ violent ("thundering roar", bang, loud explosion) and 6/ "electrical" or crackling sound ("noise like a mosquito zapper")."*

All these categories of sound are reported one or more times in Hessdalen.

Leif Havik heard sound on one occasion:

> "We hardly had enough time to stop the engine of the car before a light appeared. We jumped out of the car, like shot out of a catapult's seat - there was "our" oblong "cigar" again. It had a clear red light in the front, and it moved in a slow, undulating motion. Since it passed so close, it was possible for the first time to hear sound from it. It was a kind of hissing sound, which I can mostly compare with the sound of high voltage cables in humid weather conditions."

A hissing sound was also described by Bjarne Lillevold in connection with his observations at the Red Cross cabin at Hessdalskjølen, September 1982.

Jon Arvid says He has heard a slight sound on one occasion - when he was 15 meters from "it". The sound he heard can best be described as something close to "slow bike gears" - that is, a kind of crackling sound (as in category 6 above).

Otherwise Teodorani heard sound during the EMBLA expedition in 2000 when he, along with two others at Aspåskjølen observed one disc-shaped neon-like, yellow-white light of approximately 30-40 cm in diameter with sharp contours just at the edge of the forest 100 meters away A whistling sound could be heard when the light gradually turned on (category
3) Category 5 - violent sounds, thunder, roar and bangs - are mentioned in the book to Havik:

> "On September 6, 1984, two people heard deep rumbling and bangs at 9:18 am. and 3.25 pm. and 3.33 am. They came from the northeast. On September 7th the same year, several double strokes were heard on the west side of mount Romundhaugen The sounds around Romundhaugen sounded as if the rumbling moved around the mountain."

We've been told that deep rumbling have been heard in recent times. A family who has a cabin in Finnsådalen, has by a couple of occasions have had to cancel their stay in the middle of the night - when the kids have become terrified due to "bangs and rumbling" that came from the mountain itself - Finnsåhøgda!

Category 1 - low-frequency humming - is registered in Hessdalen also in cases without any phenomenon being observed. Among other things, we have had a lot of contact with the man who runs the Facebook page "Hessdalen light phenomenon" - Tomas Dahl. He says that he has experienced this kind of sound phenomena in Hessdalen himself - to the extent that it has been directly bothersome! The same man has also said that he has talked to people who experience such sounds constantly. For one family in Hessdalen, this buzzing sound is so intense that the kitchen table shook!

But ... this time it was just an overgrown bumblebee…

- We agree that this must be the nicest trip and the most wonderful view so far. From the top, and along the way down, we photographed eagerly.

In the evening we're back in place at Slettælet, but unfortunately it's raining. Fog lies like a thick lid all over the Øyongen area. We spend several hours without seeing anything.

The next day we decide to go home after checking the weather forecast. Rain and fog all day, evening and night.

On the way home, we discuss the observations we saw this weekend: The four lights sliding over mount Morkavollhøgda - are they of the same type that we saw four times in the Easter, and once in July? Are they the "observation UFO" mentioned by Wisth described as round or ovoid? Do they have a solid core? Are they made of metal? Something technical-mechanical, - a machine inside, behind the luminous surface?

Also: Are all phenomena in the Hessdalen part of the same overlying phenomenon, or are they separate phenomena who coexist? Teodorani, for example, asks what he calls "probes" - that is, a form of "robotic probes" - "collects" energy that is believed to exist due to the geology of Hessdalen? Does this work as a kind of "fuel"? Or are light phenomena and vehicles simply the same thing observed in different physical stages and states?

Teodorani states that most of the lights in the Hessdalen have outer plasma characteristics - but - that this is only based on analyzes of the photo-spherical surface. Teodorani emphasizes that it's impossible to see what's inside a plasma - just as we can't see what's inside a star or the sun, but just the outer photo-sphere. Similarly, only the outer photosphere of the light phenomena in Hessdalen has been analyzed at present:

> *"One cannot rule out that in the center of the light phenomena there is a solid object that has the ability to ionize itself, the surrounding air, form plasma and prevent any possibility of seeing what is inside," says Teodorani . If this is the case, the origin of the light phenomena may be an "exotic machine" that surpasses the capacity of our current technological capability - with the proviso that not a kind of top-secret "Black Project" is taking place today in deserted areas of the globe, such as Hessdalen."*

Teodorani writes "an alternative method for the scientific search for extraterrestrial intelligent life: the local SETI":

> *"The presence on Earth of explorative devices of possible exogenous origin would appear necessarily like an anomaly in our atmosphere. Such an anomaly might be possibly reported in the form of luminous phenomena in the skies of some areas of Earth, both as a transient occurrence and as a spatial and temporal recurrence. If the visiting spacecrafts or automatic probes come from civilizations that are highly more advanced than ours the anomaly that they would be able to create in our atmosphere might be of a nature that cannot be predicted at all. What presumably comes from a highly evolved science, possibly possessed by a civilization that could have earned one million of years of advantage in comparison to us, might appear like "magic" even to the eyes of our present science.*
>
> *An exogenous probe might not be necessarily something "mechanical" as we expect from our technology, but something much more exotic. Therefore, even if we are not in a condition to extrapolate the future point of a super-civilization starting from ours, we can maybe speculate on what we could see. For instance, we cannot exclude the possibility that such a master civilization is able to instruct a "plasma ball" to acquire*

> *the functions of an "intelligent probe" based on a particle neural network that is planned to work both as a multi-sensing device and as a computer. After all, our own technology, which substantially was born only two centuries ago, is starting already now to plan a new generation of computers based both on the DNA and on quantum mechanics and it is already starting to use the very sophisticated science of nanotechnology."*

I am uncertain of what Teodorani means with "particle-neural network" and" multi-sensing device" - but I assume that it's about networks capable of sending and receiving information, as well as processing data, something similar to what neurons do in the brain. In other words, Teodorani opens up that EVEN, if in individual cases it seems that some of the registered phenomena in Hessdalen may "only" be gas / plasma / ionized air and dust, and not a solid object, it can still be a type of advanced and exotic technology.

When Bjørn Gitle Hauge - employed at Østfold University College and involved in Science Camp - in one of the documentary films about Hessdalen is exclaiming "it just burned up!" it may perhaps just as easily be an example of that the plasma ball has carried out its task, - ie collected, registered and sent information - for then to annihilate itself... self-destruct? Thus, with Teodorani's approach, there are no contradiction between plasma theories and theories of intelligent control.

11 MORE "SATELLITES…"

The last weekend in August we sit and check the weather forecast. It is highly uncertain and changes for every update. We have things to do at home, and if we are going to Hessdalen this weekend we would rather have nice weather. It is, after all, a few hours to drive …

However, it's anything but starlit and clear sky when we park at Slettælet Friday night. It slopes down, fog is thick as porridge and the visibility is equal to zero. Again, it appears to be an observation night with engine, heater and wipers on. Damn! This is exactly what we wanted to avoid. Is it possible at all to observe anything under these conditions? To keep up the courage I refer to Havik who has experienced and written that "it shows up in all kinds of weather". And from the report material there are many examples of UFOs coming down through the cloud cover: Three examples from Wisth's book:

> *"… Suddenly something phosphorous came through the cloud cover just beyond mount Finnsåhøgda. Amazed, we saw this "phosphorus light" making some strange zigzag movements before it disappeared inwards the mountain.*

"... later, at 23 o'clock, we got to see it again from the" Plateau ". Then it came through the cloud cover, swept down with great speed and disappeared behind Finnsåhøgda. "

"... a shiny object came through a gap in the cloud cover. It looked like it was coming from above, but beneath the clouds it flattened out after making a "spiral motion". It continued to maneuver with strange turns until it disappeared behind the peak of mount Skarvan."

Precisely spiral movement is a strange but quite widespread characteristic of "UFO maneuvering", which surprisingly often is repeated in the reports. Internationally, this is often compared to a falling leaf - "falling leaf motion" - or as a "pendulum motion". It's often when a UFO is seen to descend towards the ground from high altitude that this movement
pattern is reported.

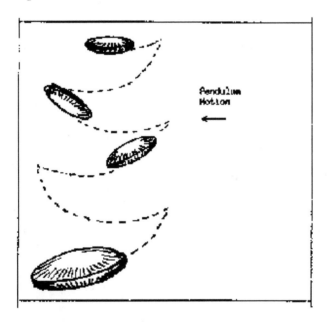

"Pendulum motion". From "The Ufo evidence" – R. Hall.

An example from Havik's book:

"The same evening at 23.20, several people saw a light sphere on the sky

> *north-northwest of Hessdalen. It jumped up and down and did remarkable movements. Then it disappeared into the forest behind some trees, then to come up again. Finally, it descended like a "falling leaf" and disappeared for good."*

However, there is little coming down through the cloud cover at Slettælet for the time being, other than rain, and the only pendulum motion so far is performed by the wipers keeping the rain away...

But what was that? A light inside the forest! Car? We're waiting... but no car appears. The light shows up and disappears several times. Are there cabin people who are out walking with a flashlight in the rain? This late? Someone with headlamps on bikes? We see yellow, white - and sometimes - a red light. Brake lights? A car driving back and forth? The light is definitely moving. Here and there, up and down too. It can't be far away, so we drive over to the forest to see. Nothing. When we return to our parking lot after a while, the light is gone.

...

We wait for another hour. Nothing more happens. We therefore decide to drive to Aspåskjølen. Maybe there's better view from there? Before we leave, I blink several times with the car head lights at the forest. At the same time we see a powerful flash slightly tilted upwards to the right of us. Could it be a kind of response?

In the 80's, it was believed that phenomena responded if they were illuminated with a powerful flashlight, for example, or if one used the head lights on a car. During the field action in 1984, one wanted to test this in more controlled forms, and used a laser. In the technical report, Erling Strand writes:

> *"We used the laser, and pointed it towards a flashing light, in two different cases, totally 9 times. 8 of these times, there was a reaction.*
>
> *In the first case, there was a regular flashing light, slowly moving towards north, on Sunday 12 February at 7.35 pm. The flashing had been regular all the time we had seen the light. The light moved slowly. From*

the first time we saw it in the south, until it disappeared in the north, it took about 15 minutes. When this light was in the northern part of Finnsåhøgda, we pointed the laser towards it for the first time. At once, it changed the flashing sequence: From a regular flashing light, it became a regular double-flashing light:

Flash.Flash.......Flash.Flash.......Flash.Flash....... *After about 10 seconds, we put the laser down, at once it became a regular single-flashing light again:* **Flash......Flash......Flash......** *After about 10 seconds we repeated this again. It was repeated totally 4 times before it went out of sight. All the times, we got this double-flashing, when the laser was pointing at it.*

The second case, the same type of light came from the north and moved towards south. It was the same day, Sunday 12 February at 8.41 pm. When the light was in the west, we pointed the laser towards it. The same thing happened now; it changed to a double-flashing light when the laser pointed towards it. This time we did it 5 times. Only the last of these times did we not get any double-flashing. But 4 of these 5 times, we got it.

The test was done like this: Kurt Persson used binoculars looking at the light. He told what he was seeing all the time; he said: "flash...flash...flash..." . I (Erling Strand) used the laser. He could not see where I was pointing with the laser. When I raised the laser, pointing at the light, he said: "flash.flash.....flash.flash.....flash.flash....." . May Britt Pellving was a witness to what we were doing. There were also other people out at that moment, but they were concentrating on their work.

As if this wasn't enough - about a week later, the following happened:

"Leif Havik was alone in the caravan. He was taking on a survival suit. Åge Moe (farmer in Hessdalen) and Edvin Kværnes (from Ålen), had just arrived at the caravan. They waited outside; Moe stood on the north side of the door to the carriage, and Kværnes waited on the south side. They were all going to the Øyungnesset, to observe from there. When Leif went out of the caravan, a red light swirled around his legs before it disappeared. Moe said, "Look at the reflex". That was the only explanation he could find at that time. Leif saw at once

> *that the light was of the same kind as the laser we used. At this time, this laser was in Oslo.*
>
> *To make sure it really was the same type of light, as from our laser, we brought the laser up again on February 25th. Moe had never seen a laser before. We took him to the caravan and it was about the same time of day. When I illuminated the snow at our feet, Moe said, "It was just what I saw! But it was a little weaker." Then I illuminated the floor of the caravan, and he said, "It was a little stronger than that". We haven't found any explanation for this light, and I don't think we will either. During a conversation, Leif said, "If only I had put my palm over it, then maybe I could see where it came from. But I didn't think about it when we saw it." A second after the light was gone, they looked straight up, but nothing was seen. It was cloudy weather, but just above the caravan there was an opening in the cloud cover, and the stars could be seen through this opening."*

We hold up a little longer, waiting for something more to appear. But nothing happens. At Aspåskjølen, it's even worse, if possible. We hardly see the forest edge a hundred meters ahead of us. There's no point. We decide to call it a night and head for the cabin.

It's still raining the next day, so we take our time eating breakfast. Later that day, we drive down to Ålen to buy lunch. We then go to Båttjønndalen Valley. There's autumn colors everywhere. Soon it will be possible to observe the "falling leaf motion" in buckets and pails.

We park and stroll along the road. Båttjønndalsveien road is also called "The summer farm road", after all the old summer farms that are around in the terrain on both sides of the road. This must represent some of the most beautiful landscape Norway has to offer, in our sincere opinion; hilly mountains, heather-covered mountain fountains, close in close with small and large mires. Through the orange and reddish-brown landscape the road winds its way, where sheep with lamb lie in the roadside, while - like us - they enjoy the rest of the summer. It's all framed by majestic mountains that are reflected in the many ponds. A natural pearl!

We walk all the way through Båttjønndalen to the little lake

Skarvtjønna in the north, turn and go the same way back. Just Skarvtjønna was the site of one of the strangest sightings in Hessdalen made ever. From the archive at hessdalen.org:

> *"On the other side of Skarvtjønna we first saw three orange lights floating over the water. The two lights in the middle turned to the sides at the same time that one stood in front of the other occasionally, it looked as if the two were part of a unit. We observed these for quite some time before I turned on my headlamp to go closer. I went approx. 30 meters to the water, but then all the lights suddenly disappeared. When I went back to the road, they came back, but this time there were five lights. They hovered over the water and moved subtly up and down, and to the sides in a synchronous manner. Sometimes one of the lights disappeared and then came back. This I suppose lasted for an hour.*
>
> *While the observation described above was going on, we saw a white light shining on us and disturbing us as we saw the five yellow lights over the lake. We thought there was a person with a flashlight. The white light appeared in the middle of the mire and lit a long way. After one of the orange lights had gone out, an orange light appeared on the right side of the road. It came close to us, - 3 meters and retired quickly when we lit it with our flashlight. Then a small white light appeared to the left of the orange, but higher up. It looked like it had flowed from the mire up onto the top of the tree. This light lit up and directed something that can remind of a small headlight in our direction. This lasted a maximum of 3 seconds. Then it disappeared.*
>
> *We both had the impression that this light was what we first thought was a person with a flashlight. Next to the orange light, there was now a small, dark blue light. Both now stood quietly a few meters above the ground. The five orange balls disappeared while this was going on. A white light reappeared high up and flashed in blue and red for a few seconds before it disappeared. The three flashes were powerful and lasted for approx. half a second each. It had been two and a half hours and we had to return. The one orange light was still hanging over the mire by Skarvtjønna when we left."*

An example of lights both close to the observers and low in the terrain... Phd. in astrophysics, Teodorani, has also had experiences with phenomena close and low in the terrain, eg. from Aspåskjølen, just in the forest edge a hundred meters away. Teodorani stated that he felt observed in connection with this incident and raised questions about whether the expedition (EMBLA 2000 field action) was perhaps under the supervision of an intelligence?

This experience, together with several other specific episodes during visits to the Hessdalen, apparently resulted that Teodorani to an extent "converted" in his view of Hessdalen and the phenomena there.

As a participant at the workshop under the auspices of Project Hessdalen 1994, and later head of the EMBLA expeditions in the early 2000s, Teodorani had a geophysical approach to the phenomena, - among other things related to stress in the bedrock, piezo electricity etc. - which is also evident in the first articles that were published. In later articles, however, the SETV hypothesis (search for extraterrestrial visitation) is increasingly emphasized.

The single incident, which might have rocked Teodorani in his view, was when he and two others saw three point-like triangular lights sliding slowly toward Aspåskjølen from the south. The lights stopped over Aspåskjølen and made a 90 degree turn. Through binoculars, Teodorani could see that the lights were attached to a dark object. The starry sky was blocked out…

On several occasions when we ourselves have been on Aspåskjølen, we have seen flashes inside Båttjønndalen… Now we're just in the center of the area where the flashes have appeared to occur most often. In the 80's, it was often here that the objects passed. From south to north, through Båttjønndalen, in front of Finnsåhøgda. One should have had a time machine and traveled back in time...

Here and now - 9:30 pm, August 25th. 2018, we're in place at Aspåskjølen. It's clear weather, starry sky and full moon. A light appears in the south. It heads right at us. Blinking! Is it a plane? I check the flight radar app, but it froze, - no network found.

Yes, right! We hear the sound of the motors, and finally the app finds network. It turns out to be the evening flight Amsterdam–Trondheim with course for Værnes airport who passes over us.

As a rule, it's never a problem to recognize aircrafts. But occasionally - as this time – planes can look fascinating in cases where they have the landing lights turned on, and are heading straight towards you.

The reason I keep an eye on the aircrafts is something Teodorani wrote in the article "EMBLA 2002 - an optical and ground survey in Hessdalen":

> *"Some strange flying devices with an apparently linear movement pattern were seen in the sky, where the anomaly consisted of the colors and the light composition which were totally outside FAA rules for aircraft; In one case, only white light was observed where the object just disappeared after a flash, and in another case, the lights were merely flashing, double red lights. Is this a result of only partially successful imitations?"*

That's exactly what Jon Arvid claims; "They" camouflage themselves. And this is something we are increasingly experiencing ourselves, and have gradually become relatively convinced of.

Slettælet.

--

It's almost starlit when we park at Slettælet eleven pm. Tonight, we've brought the coveralls. I've barely pulled up the zipper before a light appears over Morkavollhøgda. A very bright light! It appears in the same place and in the same path as last time. The light, which is yellow and shines brightly, comes in the direction of where we stand! It maneuvers a little irregularly it seems like. Flickers a bit here and there, up and down and make small pace changes. I rush into the car and get the camera. But before I reach to hit the record button, the light becomes much weaker. NOW, the light is white and pale, just barely visible, and suddenly it has a very regular path. Suddenly it became very "satellite-like". We can still follow it with the eyes, like a little dot, as it slides obliquely over us, turns and disappears beyond Lake Øyongen...

I check both satellite tracker apps on the phone, but - no - according to them there should not be satellites over Trøndelag at this moment.

Shortly after, the "same" type of light comes back, and a little later number three. But unlike the first, the lights now look "satellite-like" from the time we first saw them until they disappear.

Are these satellites? They glow lightly, and pass at high altitude... However, we clearly saw that the first didn't go high - but passed pretty low over us! In other words, it may just as well be that the distance (height) is NOT so great, but that the phenomenon "turns off the light" - as a form of "camouflage"? Again I check the apps on the phone, and again they show that there are no satellites in the nearest perimeter.

- It has been a long time without anything happening. The time is 12:45 am. Eventually, we begin to think about moving. Drive to Aspåskjølen, maybe? We haven't said it, before a huge light turns up in the direction of Båttjønndalen! Unfortunately, it's only Hege who sees it. I've bent down looking - of all things - after my cap that has fallen down. Hege says that it was almost as big as the moon. A white, bright light. And oval. She sees it for three seconds, and at that time it flashes three times. Then it disappears.

Later, when we drive through the valley, we see a light over Hegsethøgda. It's moving south, and shines stronger than Venus. It dimmers and turns into a "satellite" before I even get to think of the camera. We observe almost one hour from Aspåskjølen, but without counting results.

- The next day it's time to leave and go home. In the car, we discuss these "satellites" we have seen and whether it can be a kind of "camouflage". Are the "satellites" the same type of light as the "sailplanes" we saw in Easter - just sighted higher in the sky, - or are these two different "models"? Are both "satellites" and "sailplanes" really the same as what was referred to as "the observation UFO" in the 80s, - as described, among other things. In Wisth's book? And, can all of these types be about the (supposedly) self-replicating robotic probes Teodorani is talking about? At Slettælet we noticed that the first light appeared as a large light ball, then the light became "satellite-like" - but only after I directed the camera against it...

Teodorani about camouflage:

"If a form of "alien intelligence" is behind the phenomena in Hessdalen, this hypothetical intelligence has shown no interest in seeking direct, coherent and structured communication with humanity - but instead shown a behavior that indicates that the light phenomena must be regarded as totally elusive. Is this hypothetical intelligence worth trusting? The answer so far is no." If the development of intelligence in the universe has the sole purpose of striving for survival (and not noble considerations), it is no wonder that any foreign intelligence is not interested in communicating with us - beyond controlling our actions in such a way that we do not notice it in real time. If this is the case, the only intelligent manifestation of such a typology will be falsehood and mimicry. Therefore, the question remains open..."

Will it simply pay off to keep a low profile? Turn off the car engine, not slam with car doors, talk as little as possible and with low voices. Leave the camera and phone at the cabin, for example? We think this must be tried out the next time…

12 GETTING CLOSE IS EASIER SAID THAN DONE

Already next weekend, we start off at the information boards at Hessdalskjølen and park. There's a new pathway upwards towards Mount Rogne, and we think that there must be several potential lookout points a little up the hillside. As we talked about last time, we leave camera and cell phones in the car. Now we'll see if it can have any impact?

Can it really be as simple, and banal, that one saw more - more often and more spectacular things - in the 80's because people didn't have proper cameras and video cameras at the time? No one had smartphones either, of course. Now everyone walks around with their own small camera in their pockets…

I'm not at all convinced that the theory has any credibility - because I've experienced myself that you need to have quite *advanced* photo equipment in order to have hope of taking good pictures in the dark. Why would any alien intelligence bother with bad phone images that don't prove anything? But it's worth a try. So when we sit at dusk under the tree line at Mount
Rognefjell, we are completely "unarmed".

The view is impeccable. We look south in the valley to mount Morkavollhøgda, in the west we have view inwards Båttjønndalen valley - and right in front of us Mount Finnsåhøgda. We have barely rolled out the seat pad and sat down in the heather before we pop up again. Here comes "satellite" number 1. - high in the sky. It comes from the southeast, over mount Rogne, right above our heads as we sit. And now we see something new; It becomes suddenly much brighter - almost like a flash that lasts several seconds - then it becomes a "satellite" again. Three times in a row, this happens - three "flashes" while passing over our heads. Then it becomes a small "dot" and disappears obliquely across Hessdalslia hillside and further in the direction north towards Haltdalen. During the three long "flashes" it has a brightness equal to something midway between Venus and the full moon!

Two "satellites" come in roughly the same orbit over Rogne, but - as we experienced last weekend - NOW, they are "satellite-like" from we first see them until they are out of sight. Since the phone is left in the car, I don't have the opportunity to check the satellite tracker apps. The first one - with the three "flashes" can't possibly be a satellite as it varies that much in brightness? Three times it shines very strongly, then becomes a pale little dot.

At home I read about Iridium satellites:

> *"The Iridium satellites are the" base stations "for satellite phones. There are 66 of them in orbit around the earth, plus some in reserve. The special thing about these satellites is the antennas. The three smooth polished plates act as mirrors. Sometimes they reflect sunlight onto the earth in a powerful flash that lasts a few seconds. Some of the flashes are weak, while others are almost as bright as the full moon!"*

However, Iridium satellites only emit ONE flash, I read. Not three, as in this case. Therefore, Iridium satellite, it most probably isn't, but perhaps another, special type of satellite? A rotating satellite maybe? Or rocket? Maybe some rotating debris? An object that rotates will - in theory - emit light flashes every time a reflective surface is at the correct angle relative to the sunlight. But if this were the case, - it should have flashed both before and after the three powerful flashes we saw? Not just three powerful flashes as it passed over our heads, and that's it, nothing before or after?

- After this we sit for an hour without seeing anything. We decide to head down to the car and move inwards to Slettælet. Tonight there's not a cloud in the sky, which is good. But it's tiring to be "fooled" all the time by bright stars and flight passages. Not that we really let ourselves be fooled, but absolutely everything must be checked.

At Slettælet we're not alone, it turns out. There is a motorhome parked there. More people out in the same errand... Not long after we parked, Hege sees a powerful flash. It's big, lasts just a few seconds - and just too short for me to see it. It has clear contours and seems concentrated, says Hege. It "turns off" as when you turn off a switch. I myself keep an eye on
the horizon over Mount Morkavollhøgda. We've seen "satellites" come sliding across this mountain repeatedly now. Will this happen tonight as well? Before I'm finished thinking it, a light appears over the horizon. But this is not one of the usual "satellites". This is something else. It blinks in white. A plane?

At the same time, Hege points in the direction of a flash she has seen in the direction of Skarvan - with the mountain as a background. I lose eye contact with the white, flashing "plane" for a moment, and it's hard to spot it again. When - after a while - I see it again, I understand why; It does not flash regularly, as aircraft usually do. This "plane" flashes at irregular intervals, it seems. Something I haven't seen before. And where are the colors? Aircrafts should blink in both white, red and green:

White, blinking strobe lights, red, flashing anti-collision lights, one above and one below, and a red navigation light on the left wing, as well as a green on the right. Here it only flashes in white. And besides, doesn't it use abnormally long time to pass? I check the flight radar app, but unfortunately - no signal at the moment.

Can it be a military aircraft? There have been many speculations about possible military activity in Hessdalen over the years. Already in the beginning, in the early 1980s, it was speculated that there could be talk of a new type of spy satellite that was being tested by NATO. Just military satellites as the only explanation were probably questionable, as one observed phenomena down in the valley with the mountains as background.

But that one thought that the phenomena could be related to something military is not so strange since the authorities - apparently - did not lift a finger to find out what was going on.

Jon Arvid also mentioned that early in the 1980s, people were wondering if there could be a connection. The observations started at the same time as the new facility for the Home Guard was built in Haltdalen. Anyway, it would be strange if there was no military interest in Hessdalen? One observation is quite special in that respect. From hessdalen.org; observations 2002:

> *"Ruth Mary drove home from the store in Hessdalen. When she was just north of the community center, at Trøan, south of Hegseth, she saw a black, or gray-black "plane", without windows, down to the river. She looked down at this flying thing. It flew very low, just across the river, from north to south. The first thing she thought about was that it was a plane, because it had wings, but she thought it was so strange that it was flying so low and that it had no windows."*

In a comment to this report, Erling Strand writes:

> *"Could it have been a drone from the air force? About. 40 minutes after this observation, I (Erling Strand), Bjørn-Gitle Hauge and some other people, saw a large military aircraft flying very low in the valley."*

Possible, but quite strange with military drones all the way down to river Hesja? In other contexts, military helicopters are seen:

> *"Two helicopters from the air force were seen near mount Rognefjell, northeast of Hessdalen. The first came from Røros town and circled around Rogne before it landed near the top. Jon Aspås saw someone walking around the helicopter. After a while it left with a box or something hanging under it. Minutes later came a new helicopter in the same area, but this only passed before it returned in the direction of Røros. The air force has shown great interest in this area in recent months."(Source: Project Hessdalen Bulletin, 1983).*

In connection with the EMBLA team experiencing structured objects during the field actions in the early 2000s, Teodorani considers military activity as a possible alternative to the ET hypothesis.

I've thought of something similar myself: As previously mentioned, there existed a NATO base south of Hessdalen - at mount Hummelfjell. This was manned up to and including 1986, and had at the most 100 employees. According to newspaper articles in Røros newspaper, Arbeidets Rett, there's still military activity on the base. In addition, there existed a similar, smaller NATO base north of Hessdalen - at Bringen near Haltdalen.

Severe underground mountain facilities were blown out in connection with these bases. Between Hummelfjell and Bringen there are seven miles in airline, and the Hessdalen valley lies midway between these two stations. Could it be that Hessdalen and the surrounding area were the site of experiments under the auspices of some top secret branch of NATO?

The more I see with my own eyes in Hessdalen, the less I think that the theory has credibility. It seems otherwise unlikely that military experiments would take place for decades after decades. Some characteristics of the UFO phenomena reported from Hessdalen, - ie. light and color composition, maneuvering and pattern of movement among other things -
has also been reported internationally since 1947. If this were / is a military project, shouldn't one expect a development? A kind of UFO evolution, with ever-evolving designs and improvements in maneuvering and performance? Or is it not a matter of experimentation, but rather the stationing of exotic technology? Does Hessdalen represent a kind of hangar? A "garage" for various models of exotic vehicles? One big problem with these theories is that they are just as little testable as the ET hypothesis. We are left with assumptions and just have to guess...

At Slettælet there's not much interesting happening. Also, our companion in the motor home seems to have called it a night. We decide to follow his example and set course forward in the valley.

At Kjerringvollen, we register a bright "star" in the northwest. I slow down and stop. No, it stands still. Star or planet, we conclude, and drive on. However, I take a little look aside, just in case... Strange as it changes colors ... Now wait! Now it has come a lot closer! It is so bright! Again we stop and get out of the car. But before we reach to do anything, the light dims and disappears. It wasn't a star, and not a plane. This light also went low in the terrain, and must have been pretty close to us when it disappeared. It takes a while before we move on.

It's passed 2 am. before we return to the cabin. Before I fall asleep I think about this thing with camouflage; Jon Arvid has mentioned that "they" can both imitate stars and the moon, and Teodorani has mentioned imitations of airplane lights. We have even begun to wonder if any intelligence behind the light phenomena can operate with "satellite camouflage" too ...?

But when that is said: The whole idea of UFOs and camouflage suffers from a great paradox - because if the intention is not to be discovered; evoke the least possible attention - why then surround yourself with light at all? The best and simplest form of camouflage would have been to "turn off the switch"? "Pull out the plug"?

On the other hand, it is possible that this is precisely what we have experienced when we have seen light disappear in loose air on five occasions?

I yawn and turn off the light.

Perhaps UFOs MUST emit light because the light is a direct consequence of the propulsion mechanism itself? Again one can only guess.

- We sleep in on Saturday. After breakfast, I visit Project Hessdalens website. A new observation report has been published. This is from last Saturday, it turns out, at. 10.47 pm. When we were parked at Slettælet!

> *"Bjørn and his two sons were driving on the mountain road Setereveien. They were on their way to lake Langen, further south. On the roads last curve before Båttjønndalen, they see a big light over mount Fjellbekkhøgda. It is big, about 70% of the size of the moon. It moves fast towards the north and faded away after a very few seconds. The light could not be seen anymore. Patrick said he could see a black object where the light had been. The light had one strong light in the front, and a smaller light in the back. These were connected with parts of a circle. This observation made a great impression on the observers."*

Hege also saw a large light in the direction of Båttjønndalen last Saturday, but this was later in the evening ... After a short trip down to Ålen, we set course towards Båttjønndalen ourselves. We're aiming towards the top of Mount Båttjønnhøgda. We are a bit unlucky with the choice of route, and get a rather steep and tiring ascent. But the view from the top is worth the effort. The Hessdalen mountains never disappoints in that way!

Down by the car, we look out a mountain cliff nearby. Wouldn't it be a perfect vantage point for tonight? The cliff is not so far from the road, and to achieve a similar view we have to go a long way up the mountainside. We also assume that the motorhome that was parked on Slettælet yesterday will be in place tonight as well, which we suppose will reduce the chances of seeing something from there.

While Hege is in the shower, I'm googling randomly. I come across a NRK feature I can't remember having seen before. The entry is from Science Camp 2016. Bjørn Gitle Hauge at the Østfold University College is interviewed here. In the episode he comes with some concessions that are unusual coming from him; he says that the residents of Hessdalen have been right all the way! - Several of their stories can now be confirmed, says
Hauge - among other things; descriptions of two lights together as "dancing around" in the sky as if they were playing, or three lights together that follow each other in a triangle formation. At the same time, Hauge maintains that the solution lies in the geophysical conditions in Hessdalen. - It has been looked upwards too much, he says. - We have to look downwards.

It's a mystery to me how Hauge in one moment can talk about light that follows each other in triangle formation, and in the next moment talk about supposed geophysical reasons for this. It doesn't coincide. Such things cannot arise entirely by themselves in nature?

Anyway, - at least it is positive for Hessdalens residents that Hauge finally confirms at least SOME of their stories, I think.

One of the reasons I would like to enter Båttjøndalen Valley this evening, is the desire to get closer to the phenomena. See it as close as possible - to see *behind* the light. What is it that shines? What is the source?

However, we know that this is easier said than done. Already in 1982, Arne P. Thommassen said that it seemed that the phenomena operated with a certain minimum distance for how close it was possible to come. - We have wondered a lot, and are wondering why, said Thomassen at the time.

Jon Arvid told us that he was inside Båttjønndalen skiing in the nights of the 80s. He went back and forth at the foot of Finnsåhøgda. But getting close to them was easier said than done; - "They probably knew I was there, says Jon Arvid."

8.15 pm we find the lookout point at the cliff, and take on our coveralls. From here we have a view of the mountains to the west, while Båttjønndalen valley with all its small and large lakes lies in front of us to the north-east. In the back we have the dark silhouette of mount Rogne. What was that? A white flash to the left of Rogne? There it was again!
Behind Rogne... - can there be car headlights? Hege has also become aware now. Again it flashes. At the same time, we see something like a headlamp, or like a car - a sweeping light, as a car would do in a curve.

Ok, it must be car headlights we're watching. There is a toll road from Ålen, over the mountain, to Tydal as far as I know. Possibly lights from the road are visible from our position? Presumably, there must be light from the mountain pass we see, but we are wondering about the brightness in relation to the distance...

After having said us somewhat satisfied with this explanation, we turn around and observe south-west for a period. Sometimes I glance over my shoulder in the direction of mount Rogne.

It continues to flash around Rogne, I can see. Blue-white small and large flashes. But, hey! Now it's light in FRONT of Rogne! It's definitely a yellow, smaller light that is moving in front of the mountain. Now we're immediately more eager. We know there is no car road up in mount Rogne, at least. We have even gone up the mountain side, both on skis and on foot, sweared in the deep snow, lit bonfire, grilled sausages and drank coffee. So we should be well acquainted with the terrain.

The light goes back and forth, up and down, all the time in front of the mountain. Both around the top and far down in the mountainside. We also register something searchlight-like. A beam of light goes in different directions. Occasionally the beam is pointing straight up! Can there be people there with powerful headlamps? Eager exercisers out for a late night session? In that case, they must be many, scattered all over the mountain and in extremely good shape. The light is moving here and there, at a great pace.

It has probably been going on for approx. half an hour now. Sometimes the light is gone, then it comes back. Is it moving behind the mountain as seen from our angle? At times we only see blue-white flashes, then we see the yellow, moving light again. At the same time, Hege sees a small flash in the edge of the forest by the little lake to the right of us. It's white,
concentrated and stronger than a flashlight, she says.

Ok, now there is a lot to pay attention to... There is still activity around Rogne, and simultaneously we keep an eye on the lake. In the corner of the eye, Hege sees something lit up in the edge of the forest again. After this she is looking straight at the lake. Suddenly a round blue light appears in the middle of the lake. A blue, illuminated circle, approx. 2 meters in diameter. It's a strong blue color, which decreases. The whole thing only lasts a few seconds, then the luminous ring is gone.

After this, Hege is scared. The lake is only max. 200 meters from us. It feels anything but comfortable to be so close to it, she says. Hege wants to return to the car. I'm staring intensely at the lake, but all I see is the dark night.

Before we go, I blink with my headlamp in the direction of the lake, but nothing happens. In the car we talk a little about the experience. We remember what Ruth Mary said – two hundred meters is quite close, - at least when you don't know WHAT you're close to... We must have respect, we think. We don't know what this is and what the h*** we're doing.

We drive what the Toyota can considering the gravel road to Vårhuskjølen, excited about whether the lights around Rogne are still there, or whether the "performance" is over. We park and rush out of the car. A few minutes goes ... THERE! A flash, and another. So there is still something going on up in the mountainside on the other side of the valley. I take out the camcorder and records for several minutes but register no light while the camera is
turned on. We are uncertain whether the "activity" has ceased, but we decide to drive to the Red Cross cabin up on Hessdalskjølen, in other words - at the foot of mount Rogne, hoping to get right close to what might still be there. We park and leave the car, stare up the mountain side.

A station wagon comes up Hessdalslia hill, stops and stands still in the middle of the main road. Seems like those who sit inside the car also stare up the mountainside. Nothing strange about that - as there has been activity around Rogne now, for over an hour, - apparently both in front and behind the mountain, - this must also have been visible to the population down in Ålen. Maybe also for people living in Haltdalen? We stay at Hessdalskjølen for half an hour. During this time, we both believe that we see a slightly smaller, faint flash about halfway up the mountainside. Nothing more is happening, so we agree to call it a night. It has been an intense evening, and we are both exhausted. We return to the cabin and fall asleep before our heads hits the pillow.

13 FOOLED!

A week later I receive an e-mail from project manager Erling Strand. This is a response to amail I sent him a while ago, describing what we saw at Easter time. Strand is a busy man, but now he has finally had time to review his inbox, and to update and post new observations on the Project Hessdalen website. He wonders if he can post the pdf file I sent him. Of course - I agree to that - and at the same time tell him that we are going to Hessdalen on Friday. Strand says there are several people in Hessdalen this weekend; a group that calls themselves "We who like Hessdalen" on facebook is supposedly in the valley all weekend. Strand thinks they have their own camp at Slettælet.

When we at dusk drive up to Slettælet, we see that it is correct. "Our" parking lot is *thoroughly* occupied; here are campers, tents and caravans scattered all over the area. In the middle of the area there are about twenty people sitting around a huge bonfire. We're considering to go over and say hello, but leave it. Don't want to be intrusive, either. We can probably come back tomorrow and ask if they've seen something, we think. Now we're eager to get ourselves in position to possibly observe something ourselves.

Again we turn off at the exit from the road, pass Vårhuskjølen, down into Finnsådalen Valley, and up the curves to Båttjønndalen Valley.

What are the lights between the birch trees? There's no cabin in any

case. We know that, because here we have driven so many times both in the dark and in daylight. Is it a bonfire? We see a yellow-orange light, maybe a little red as well. There are some white lights too.... What in the world is this? I take out my camcorder and start filming. I zoom in on
the lights, - use the camera as binoculars. I can see that the trees around are lit. The distance to the lights cannot possibly be greater than 300 meters. Whatever this is, the lights are on the ground. Is it a kind of "landing" we are looking at?

But, hey! There's something that is moving around the lights. With full zoom on the camcorder, I clearly see something moving. Figures, apparently. Are there people over there? Pilots and crew? "Small guys", with big, black eyes and long arms...? My thoughts spins around some UFO books I've read. Spectacular and dramatic cases from the United States, etc.

While my imagination is running wild, the yellow-orange light becomes weaker and eventually completely gone. The white lights also disappear soon after. Now it's just black night again in the forest. We're talking hefty while we later drive up the last couple of short steep sections, and continue on further inwards Båttjønndalen.

At lake Langen we become aware of a light from a cabin; - or rather; - something we *believe i*s cabin lights. Neither of us can remember having seen a cabin in this place before. Can we possibly see all the way to the opposite side of lake Øyongen from here? But the light seems too strong to be nearly a mile away?

It seems to be spherical like a ball and glows yellow. We drive to the parking lot, turn around and drive back. Well, the light is still there. Apparently it hovers over lake Langen. Or has it come a little closer now? It seems bigger? We leave the car, take out the camera and start filming. It goes a few minutes. The light stays in the same place. Is it light from a cabin anyway? - Yes, it probably must be... but, - it flashed! We're staring intensely towards the light - where it is now completely dark. There it comes back, - and disappears again. This happens about 3–4 times. Eventually, after a few more minutes, the light disappears completely.

Cabin lights do not flash! And don't disappear in thin air? We have many questions, but few answers when we get in the car and drive forward through Båttjønndalen and down to Vårhus.

At midnight we park at Aspåskjølen. A bright star captures our attention for a while, but is quickly revealed as the star of Capella using the app - the sixth clearest star in the sky according to Wikipedia.

We sit for almost two hours without seeing anything, and begin to think about the cabin and our sleeping bags. Then, - suddenly it flashes up in Finnsådalen! Under the horizon. Not just once, but a number of times. White, or blue-white flashes. There are minutes between each flash, and they seem to be moving around. This can't be far from the place we saw the "landing" earlier tonight? Occasionally, the light is constant and can be seen for several seconds in a row.

I leave the car and start recording, but no flashes appears while the camera is on. Besides, it's ice cold wind on Aspåskjølen, so I hurry myself into the car again. There it flashes again! Again I leave the car and record. No flash, so I get in again. This procedure repeats itself 2-3 times. Eventually it becomes longer and longer between each flash, and around two o'clock
it seems that the activity ceases altogether.

Actually, we should drive up to Finnsådalen to check, but none of us can bare the thought of that. Back at the cabin we are so tired, that just brushing our teeth becomes an effort.

- Instead, we drive up to Finnsådalen on Saturday morning. We want to examine the forest edge where we saw the lights from yesterday to possibly see if there are tracks. We find the place we stopped, cross the stream and start looking. Nothing so far. We're spreading to be more efficient...

Hege is however greeted by a Bird hunting dog with an orange vest... Hm ...!? Then she sees a green tree tent...

- Two grouse hunters have camped - of all places - over there in the woods!

Brave to light fires in the crush-dry heather kilometers from the nearest water source! Possible they had primus? The light from yesterday could resemble that. Headlights can explain the white light we saw. Possibly the dog had headlamp too?

Damn! We continue without much being said in the car... Alright! Here we were fooled. Nothing to do about that...

Now we want to make sure that there's no cabin at Langen with "proper location" in relation to the light from yesterday.

What the...! Sure there is a cabin up on the cliff on the other side of the lake! Could it really have been light from that one we saw? In the evening we drive back to Langen again and the suspicion is confirmed. Again it shines on the other side of the lake, just as yesterday. We drive to the cabin, and surely there is a car parked there too...

But the light we saw yesterday was flashing? Repeatedly! Was it something that passed in front of the light? Someone who went outside? At the WC, maybe? Or out to pick up firewood? At one kilometer distance in otherwise dumb darkness it might seem like a flash if something or someone passes in front of the light source?

But in the end, the light was completely gone? It disappeared in thin air... Well, probably they extinguished the light and simply went to sleep? Damn again!

We get in the car and drive north. We pass the cliff we sat on last weekend, but since it's raining heavily for the moment, it isn't very tempting to observe from there. According to the weather report, it will stop raining around 11 pm. Until then we stay in the car.

At lake Båttjønna we suddenly see that large parts of the lake are illuminated, - something that automatically makes us think of the ring of light Hege saw at Lake Synnertjønna last weekend. Two beams of light sweeps over the terrain, back and forth, and then straight towards us. However, when we drive a little further in the road, two silhouettes appear on the marsh. This must certainly be people with headlamps - strong headlamps - mind you. We are blinded! They shine stronger than the headlights on a car!

I don't like this. Was it these two we were watching from Aspåskjølen last night? Were people running around in Finnsådalen with headlamps of one million lumen? We do, however, doubt that there should be people who ran around up there underneath the mountain in the middle of the night. Why in the world would anyone do that? What did they have to do there? Still, it cannot be ruled out that there were people with headlamps on the ferry, - ergo, the events of last night enter into the series of uncertain observations... Heck! It should almost be forbidden to walk around with such strong headlights in Hessdalen on evenings and night times!

But we must try to learn from this. It's obviously easy to be fooled, even by the most banal things, obviously. Before we get excited, we must check all possible explanations; be it planes, stars, bright planets, satellites - *and* cabin lights, headlamps etc. etc. If all this can be excluded, one can, maybe, begin to think of unknown phenomena.

That being said; I really feel that this is exactly what we do when we check up against Flight Radar 24 (for airplanes), Starlight (for stars and planets), and Satellite Tracker (low-going satellites, and various space debris). Maybe we should be entrepreneurs? Develop our own app for detecting cabin lights and headlamps...?

The weather gets us in a better mood. The fog is gone, and when we eventually park on Aspåskjølen it is starlit. In addition, there is a lot of northern lights to see. A beautiful sight. However, there is little else to look at. It's 2 am, and it's getting shorter and shorter time between each yawn.

Suddenly - out of nowhere - a huge light right in front of us! It only lasts a few seconds; a predominantly green light with some blue and red. Most of all, it reminds us of a New Years eve rocket - a very powerful one. In the core it's red. Around the red it's blue, and outermost it's surrounded by green light. The tail is also green, and it also emits a green light that lights up in the area for a moment. It looks as if it "drips" a little green light from it before it disappears. The red, blue and green light has a clear delimitation. That said, it reminds us most of fireworks, but we don't hear any explosion. "The rocket" does not explode, as fireworks usually do. If this is fireworks, then it must have come from underneath Finnsåhøgda. Are there any pranksters at the foot of Finnsåhøgda laughing at us this minute? Someone with a self-designed rocket, in case, - for something similar we've never seen.

It is probably unlikely that anyone would shoot fireworks from a mountain in the middle of the night - just to fool us! If so, should we feel honored? But this will probably be a bit to overestimate our own significance, we feel... One need to be critical, but one must not lose ones head either.

Hege is happy that I also saw it this time. The color and size reminds a lot about the green light she saw in the Easter. It also lasted only a few seconds. This time - however - we both saw it clearly, and for her it's a relief.

14 "KNUD"

Fourteen days later, there's a warning of extreme weather that dominates the weather forecasting services. The hurricane "Knud" ravages in Western Norway, and we are supposed to get our share of this here in Trøndelag also this weekend; red triangles warn us of both extreme wind, unusually heavy rainfall, great landslide danger and so on... Hopefully we avoid the worst in the inner parts of Norway, - it's mostly out to the shore it hits? It's a matter of being an optimist, I say, while the windscreen wipers are busy keeping away the rain whipping over the windshield.

Half past seven, we arrive at the cabin. I carry our luggage from the car while Hege unpacks. The cabin is cold as ice. It's warmer outdoors than indoors. Soon to be out of firewood as well, I see when I visit the woodshed - fortunately we have an agreement with the people up on the farm for new delivery. The winter is coming up early here, and the snow is probably not very far away.

After eating and getting warm, we wait for it to be dark outside. To kill time, we put on a radio documentary we have come across from 1990. It's an excellent program! Tore Strømøy - then employed by NRK radio - took the trip to Hessdalen, went around and interviewed several of the residents. A number of observations are referred. Also - for me - completely unknown issues, older than the most intensive period in the 80s.

In the program, it's also clear that the Hessdalen residents - in the aftermath of all the ridicule they were faced with - eventually chose to shut up, and holding new observations for themselves.

Leif Havik - author of the book from 1987 - and also participant under Project Hessdalens field actions in 84 and 85, is also interviewed by Strømøy. He states that it's a pity that new observations are not reported - important information is lost - but at the same time he says that he understands the Hessdalen residents, as they have been treated badly in the media, in addition to various "experts" that have launched several "theories" - the one more unlikely than the other.

--

- It goes towards a darker season, and already around eight o'clock we turn off the road at Vårhus in the direction of Båttjønndalen Valley. Tonight we don't see trace of grouse hunters. "Knud" scares effectively most people from applying any outdoor life this weekend. But when that is said, the weather is surprisingly good at the moment. It has stopped raining, and the cloud cover is breaking up. But it's windy, and the clouds have a violent speed.

It's full moon, and this casts a miraculous reflection across Lake Båttjønna. To the right of the moon, over Skarvan, a bright light appears. A red light. It moves! Or is it the speed of the clouds around that makes it look like the light is moving? I check with the Starlight app on the phone. Could it be a planet? Yup! It's Mars that has risen above the horizon. "The Red Planet".

Later in the evening we park at Slettælet. I try to stay out of the car at first, but quickly retreat. Here it's windy from all sides! Slettælet is an open place. Here there's no shelter. Eventually the rain comes too. It probably will not be possible to see anything at all. We give up and drive to the cabin.

--

- The first thing we do after breakfast Saturday is to check the weather forecast. It reports about dry weather throughout the day, and less wind than first notified. Good news! We start to run out of new mountain peaks to climb, and in this weather we agree that mount Rogne - which we have been up to several times already - is a suitable destination for the day.

At the top it's stormy. Fresh! In fourteen days from now this year's Science Camp will be held. I do not envy those who will stay in a tent at the base of Rogne!

Down in the car, we need to drive down to Ålen to buy some supplies. On the trip down Hessdalslia hill I think of NRK's radio documentary again. Torbjørn Dragmyrhaug is one of the interviewees. Several of the observations mentioned in the program are also reproduced in Wisth's book:

> *"The most remarkable happened in daylight approx. 4:30 pm Torbjørn and Hallgerd came from Hessdalen down to Ålen. The road is very winding there, and Torbjørn had to concentrate on driving. Hallgerd had to lean forward and look up through the front window of what she discovered. - It was big like a plane and silver. No windows I could see where "it" slipped over us maybe a hundred yards away. It was rather pointy in front, and at the back I think it was some elevation. How long I saw it, I'm not sure. Maybe a minute. When we finally stopped, it had disappeared over the mountain."*

Two others who were traveling from Hessdalen down to Ålen, were Ole Bendheim and his son Petter on 24 / 10-1982, at 3.40 pm. This observation is also mentioned in the documentary, and reproduced in Wisth's book:

> *"The object came sliding down the mountain and disappeared for a moment at the edge of the forest. There it was somehow hovering over a plant field. It looked as if its length covered the entire plant field. As we could see, the "thing" stood just three to four hundred yards away from us. It must have been twice as big as a truck. The son Petter thinks it was even bigger. The object slid slowly over. Elongated, silvery, and in the front. . . Wasn't there something that moved there? In front of the*

> *object it looked as if there was a "sink" in the hull. Was it transparent there? Did they see through the object at this point? Was it the forest in the background they saw move? Or was there something inside the vehicle that moved? Bendheim has thought about this over and over. - The sight was so amazing that we might have forgotten to study details, he says. The object disappeared behind a ridge, and we didn't see it again."*

It's part of the story that Bendheim was subsequently consulted and questioned by the norwegian Air Force regarding his experience.

We for our part do not see anything sensational - neither on the trip down nor up Hessdalslia hill - and are avoiding interrogation, at least…

We drive down to the farm and ask about fire wood. It can be arranged. - At the same time, we ask if they know anything about winter clearing of Øyongsveien road? There has been talk of keeping the road open during the winter, we've heard, and in that case it would have been great news for us, - who would like to take us to Slettælet by car also after the first snowfall. However, they've not heard anything more about it, and it hardly becomes
a reality this winter in any case.

The weather forecast shows that it will be snowing next week. - There hasn't been snow in September for many years, the farmers say. It won't be staying anyway, they reassure us. Good to hear! We hope to have the opportunity to drive by car into the mountains for many weekends throughout the autumn.

What is absolutely certain is that the road through Båttjønndalen becomes impassable soon, - so we want to utilize the opportunity while we still have it.

7 pm we cross river Hesja and drive up the winding road to Vårhuskjølen. Here it's so steep that it's tiring just to be a passenger, says Hege. Above Vårhuskjølen there's a magnificent sight! An explosion of autumn colors in the sunset. However, the only "light phenomenon" is the rainbow. There are some raindrops in the air, but as long as the fog stays away - as it probably does due to the wind

- we won't complain. We drive through Båttjønndalen valley without seeing anything strange, and again we set the course for Slettælet.

It's full moon - like at Easter - comments Hege. She doesn't like sitting with her back to the moon, she says, asking me to turn the car over. The experience of the big, yellow light – in the middle of the valley - is still fresh in her memory. In the Easter, she believed that this observation was so special and unusual, that she dismissed it as an optical illusion; - It had to be something else, she thought. In retrospect, she understands that her sighting is not unique at all. On the website of Prosjekt Hessdalen we're reading that Bjørn Lillevold had a similar experience quarter past nine in the evening ninth January 2015:

> *"Bjørn drove from Hessdalen towards Ålen. When he had reached the second curve in Hessdalslia hill, he saw a huge light in the north. As big as the moon. The light was between the tunnel in Svølja and Aspås. The brightness was huge, much, much stronger than the moon. After approx. 10 seconds the light turned off."*

Something similar is also mentioned in NRK's radio documentary;

> *"Per Moen woke up in the middle of the night and saw a large, yellow light through the bedroom window. It looked like the moon in color and size, but the moon was in the opposite direction of the sky."*

A car passes our parking lot and stops at the end of Slettælet. It seems like they stop to observe. Do they see something? We scan the sky and the horizon, but can't see that there should be anything to react to. Hope it's not the moon they're watching? It has disappeared behind a cloud, but shines partly through it and illuminates the cloud cover. Hessdalen "for dummies"?

Before we call it a night we take the usual trip up to Aspåskjølen. It's still windy, but otherwise the visibility is good and parts of the sky are starlit. We want to see "the real deal" - something that the participants in the radio program tell about.

Maybe we've already seen it? The four lights with a steady path across the valley that just disappeared in the Easter, as well as the single light we saw on our way down to the cabin in July - what if we saw this up close? About. 300 meters or closer? Would we then see that it's a solid object inside the light? A solid object in metal, such as the participants in the NRK documentary tell about?

Seeing something in the daytime - which sweeps all the doubts aside - is much to request. Such observations are extremely rare. But maybe we can hope to see something in category three, as Erling Strand describes it; several lights that act together as they follow each other as if they were attached to an object? So far there's only one time in the Easter, where we
saw the two lights that stood vertically for each other and dimmed down synchronously, which can be counted under this category.

Last weekend we stood at Aspåskjølen, we saw this green "rocket" - a great light - but we didn't become any wiser after this observation. There was nothing about this observation which meant that this was something mechanical or that there was a technology behind it. On the contrary, it reminded more of a kind of unknown natural phenomenon. Spectacular, but natural. At the same time, a hypothetical, intelligent presence can be so exotic and advanced that any manifestation of it will appear completely unpredictable and incomprehensible, and not represent something we as observers "expect" or are able to recognize as technology. Especially if we only see fragments of the "technology" over a very limited time. Maybe we just see "sparks" or "exhaust" after the "machinery"?

After being fooled - not just once, but twice last week - and not seen the twist of the phenomenon this weekend, I'm a bit mistrustful on departure this Sunday. But next time it's the autumn holiday... maybe then?

As we leave Hessdalen this time, the mountain peaks are white. Looks like we should switch over to winter tires, and pack some extra warm clothes for the next weekend.

15 FLASH

We drive up Gauldalen Valley to the sound of winter tires Friday October 5th. I've just taken autumn vacation and come straight from work. As we drive through Haltdalen, Mount Rognefjell comes to view. It's white around the top, we see.

This weekend, Science Camp starts in regi of the Østfold University. The students arrive at Hessdalen by bus tonight, and have headquarters at the community center. In addition, three mountain peaks will be manned, including the new research station at Mount Skarvan, - for two full weeks ahead.

It's starlit when we turn into Slettælet 8 pm. We have barely parked before Hege sees a big flash in the south-west direction, towards lake Elgsjøen. Immediately afterwards I see it as well; a bright flash of light that illuminates the entire sky - like a silent explosion of blue-white light.

Flashes of this type we haven't seen since November last year, - only the smaller, pointwise flashes. These are far more powerful!

Suddenly, it shines pink-white around us. 360 ° - front, back and the side! Were we just inside the flash - in the center of a flash? Hege says it felt like being photographed - a blitz right in the face! We see more powerful flashes. 4-5 times. The sky and the landscape light up. They seem to come from Båttjønndalen valley now. We decide to drive in there to see where the flashes come from if possible.

We jump in the car and take off from the Slettælet. On our way down to Fjellheim we see two additional flashes. Wow! Almost like New Year's Eve! This must get both the Science Camp folks and the residents in Hessdalens attention? I give gas. Again, we take off the road at Vårhus. Driving over Vårhuskjølen we see several powerful flashes over Mount Finnsåhøgda and Mount Fjellbekkhøgda. This *has* to get captured by the alarm camera in the Blue Box?!

We park in the area between Lake Langen and Lake Båttjønna. The flashes originate from behind the mountains, we see. The most powerful behind and above Mount Båttjønnhøgda. White, yellow, blue and green flashes - like explosions. During the evening we have probably seen 20 flashes of the type that illuminates the whole sky. Eventually, it gets longer between
each flash. We stay for another hour without anything more happening.

Then we return to Slettælet. At the top of the last hill up Road Øyongsveien - before Slettælet - we see a strong light over Mount Rødhovde. Is it Mars that has moved that much during the evening? No, it can't be. Mars is in the south and is also below the horizon now. What's this? We park and leave the car. From Slettælet it is 6-7 kilometers over to Rødhovde. Hege wants me to get the camera and start recording... I think that even though this isn't Mars, it is definitely another planet... or bright star.

But ... now it's in *front* of the mountain ?! We clearly see the light against the dark silhouette of Mount Rødhovde? I pull out the camera...

There is another car parked at Slettælet tonight. Are they Dutch, possibly? They are also pointing and staring in the direction of Rødhovde. Before I get the light in focus, it has disappeared over the horizon behind the mountain. The Dutch next to us are discussing loudly without us getting hold of what they say in the gusts. I don't

understand Dutch either.
However, we understand what one of them utters in that he hurries into the car and slams the car door behind him: "Brrrrr!" Don't need dictionary for that...

I'm not sure what I've actually seen. It all went so fast that I never really managed to make any real observation. But it wasn't an airplane, nor a star or a planet - all the time the light was below the horizon of the mountain...

- What are these flashes we've seen all night, which can be reminiscent of explosions in the way they light up the whole sky and the landscape? Are these electric phenomena, as a
result of static electricity generated in the area, building up around the mountain peaks, - until energy discharges occur? Or is it rather - as some "alternative" theorists claim – that Hessdalen is a kind of "portal", and that such flashes of light are an expression of the fact that passages are "opening" and "closing". Does light flashes occur in connection with
"arrival and departure"? One report is interesting in that way:

> *"It was in the evening, and I saw something I thought was a star between the trees. Suddenly I saw that it disappeared and drove after it on snow scooter. Then "it" appeared again. It stood still and somehow pulsed. Then came a powerful flash that lit up the area, and then it was gone. The object just disappeared before my eyes." (Wisth, 83)*

The previously mentioned Arne P. Thommasen was actively involved as a photographer in Project Hessdalen in the 80s. In 1989 he published a novel - "The Geilo-bomb" - where parts of the action "took place" in Hessdalen. Although this is fiction, the author's considerations about Hessdalen - and thoughts about what was going on there in the 80s - clearly emerged.
In the book, Hessdalen is an "extraterrestrial base", - and Thomassen writes:

> *"The work with the base began in December 1981 and led to a veritable record wave of UFO observations. In the beginning, intensive investigations of the terrain were made, down to great depths. This led to*

both many and remarkable observations, especially as the ships were exploring Hessdalen itself, and huge ghostly objects sneaked around the barns and houses and frightened the wits of anyone. Three years later, the actual construction period was completed, and then the number of observations dropped sharply.

Actually, no cavity was built in the usual sense. Because the work was carried out in the 6-dimensional energy time frame, and since the base was sub-energy related to the shadow space, it was in some way not there. It was only connected to our universe through the crystal corridors. Put another way, they were there in
Hessdalen, though not in our plan, if we think of ourselves as two-dimensional
creatures. To get into their plan, the crystal channels were needed. For the layman, it could look as if the base's atoms floated between the atoms of the mountain, but this is of course a rough simplification and rather misleading. One thing is certain – it would not have been any use to locate the base with seismic or depth drilling. Thus, no ordinary tunnels went to the surface, but large homogenized crystalline mineral veins. It was preferably quartz in those veins. When the ship stopped and tilted with the bow down, a shock zone was struck in the ship's nose, which harmonized and relativized the electric fields of the quartz molecules so that they did not repel the
ship's atoms. The base in this way was quite large and spacious, with many "rooms". Since quartz is a mineral that often occurs around old mines and quarries, it was usually here that one saw the UFOs. It was here that they went down into the mountain sphere...

Every time a larger ship hitted the shock zone and penetrated into the mountain sphere, the residents of Hessdalen could notice small tremors and
powerful flashes of light. The flashes of light could sometimes range from horizon to horizon in strange broad bands of white light. But these were just innocent side effects, piezo-resonance from the shock zone. And everything became a habit over time. Most had seen much tougher issues than this, and soon there was no one who reacted to any light flashes over Mount Rognefjell or behind Mount Finnsåhøgda."

"Energy Time", " sub-energy", "shadow room", "crystal corridors"...

strange, seemingly constructed words. Still, it gives some kind of meaning. Maybe Thomassen is on to something?

For how solid is a mountain really? In fact, a rock consists mostly of empty space. Between the atoms of which the stone is built, it's a distance - relatively speaking - as between the stars in the galaxy, - the size taken into account!

Thomassen is an electrical engineer as well, and "has for many years been engaged in studies of hidden energies, hypertension, super-space and cosmic consciousness" as it says at the inner book cover.

- The first thing I do Saturday morning is to check the alarm pictures from Blue box at hessdalen.org. Nothing! Just a few planes and something that is probably a planet. How is it possible? I was almost certain that the alarm camera would capture these flashes - especially those over Finnsåhøgda - right in front of the Blue Box. It has captured similar phenomena earlier. Some of these are on youtube. On these films, however, there were several consecutive flashes, with only seconds apart. There was at least half a minute between each of the flashes we saw yesterday. Occasionally five to ten minutes or more. Could that be why the Blue Box has not caught it? Didn't the alarm camera react? Wasn't it enough time for the video recorder to start?

Hege has had some contact with Tomas Dahl through text messages. She tells him about the flashes from yesterday. Tomas, like us, questions why no alarm images exist. This should have been captured? Tomas also reminds us of the NATO exercise in Trondelag - Trident Juncture - which is underway.

Yes, we are aware of it. But we're 100% sure that the flashes from yesterday had nothing to do with "normal" military activity. In addition, I've seen maps with plans for the activity in the coming weeks. In the Gauldalen area, it looks like it's mostly transport that'll go on. The core area of activity seems to be farther south, and the start of the most intensive activity, in a few weeks.

Tomas says he should inform the Science Camp people about our observations. Strange, by the way, that no one involved in Science Camp so at least some of this yesterday? Possible they were busy with logistic and preparations at the community center? Not sure they were outdoors at all yesterday? But what about people living in Hessdalen? Must have been more than us who registered this, or did they all sit and watch Idol on TV behind the curtains?

Almost as it should be impossible to *not* see any of this as it flashed and went on for several hours!

We drive down to Ålen, shop and fill petrol on the car. At dusk we drive into Båttjønndalen. It's minus 1 degree, and clear weather. Up the steep curves in Finnsådalen Mars appears in the south, still going strong. Using the Starlight app we locate Jupiter and Uranus as well. In addition, Saturn and Neptune should be up, but we'll probably need a telescope to see them? Venus and Mercury are below the horizon...

We turn around and drive to Slettælet. The Dutch from yesterday are in place tonight as well in 2 x rental cars. Today they have coveralls, we see. Smart choice! The wind is perhaps even stronger than yesterday. They have several cameras on tripod placed around. Best to be careful when I back and park in the dark, - this photo equipment doesn't look cheap!

It seems to be lots of high tech inside the cars as well. PCs and spectrographs, possibly? Is that a radar antenna on the roof of one car?!

We're not that advanced. Beyond our phones, the most high-tech we have is cheap binoculars bought at Clas Ohlson... Not for that; I would've liked to have both a spectrum analyzer, a radar and an infrared camera, but I really think it would be a hassle. It's stressful enough to check the apps for aircrafts, satellites and stars/planets on the phone constantly. You need to have time to actually observe too, not just look at screens and gadgets? They also destroy my night vision!

But despite intact night vision, there's little or nothing to see tonight.

We really don't become any wiser about the phenomenon; yesterday we had 20+ observations in category 1: powerful light flashes that illuminated the whole sky. Today we see zilch. And where are the "satellites"? In August, we saw "satellites" in the east and west as flashed and blinked irregularly. Now they are suddenly all gone !? Strange.

Could it be that the phenomenon occurs periodically? A kind of concentration of activity? It can almost seem like this; in the easter we saw these "sailplanes": luminous balls (?) that came "sailing" over the valley to subsequently disappear into loose air. We saw this four times in the Easter. Then we didn't see it again until the end of July.

In November last year we saw two such explosion-like flashes. Then it has almost gone a year, - until we saw it more than twenty times last night. We saw these "satellites" in August. Lots of them! Now they have disappeared without a trace. Maybe they will come back in a new "period" later? Jon Arvid has said that "what was here in the 80's is more or less gone", - implicitly that the objects - the vehicles - as they saw plenty of at that time - even during the day - there have been fewer observations of lately. Perhaps these also will come back in a new "period"?

--

- Sunday we sleep until late. We check the log at sciencecamp.no. No observations there either. We stop by at Jon Arvid's place, but he's not home. It was as we thought; he is probably busy with moose hunting this weekend.

It's lovely autumn weather, so we drive in to Lake Øyongen and go for a walk. It feels like walking around in a painting; the lake itself is deep, dark blue, surrounded by mires, birch forests and heather-clad cliffs in yellow, orange, brown and red. Around us, on all sides, blue-gray mountains rise, white on the peaks, in contrast to the blue sky. We snap photos right and left.

This landscape photographing has a dual purpose as well. It has happened, up to several times, that alleged phenomena have appeared

on such photos - in broad daylight! There are several who have taken countless landscape photos, and later viewed the pictures on the PC at home - zoomed in - and apparently discovered metallic objects in the sky in various sizes and shapes. We have looked at our pictures at home on the PC as well, but so far we have not registered anything beyond things that most probably are insects or birds
etc.

A Frenchman, on the other hand - Pierre Beake - was in Hessdalen in 2015. He took hundreds of random pictures of the landscape, and on one of them, one can - zoomed in - see something that clearly looks like a flying saucer!

Project Hessdalen published the picture, and also another of a cigar-shaped object - also in daylight - and immediately met criticism for this. The images obviously had to be a hoax? However, the following year, in September 2016, previously mentioned Tomas Dahl also photographed an apparently metallic object inside Lake Øyongen. In other words; two partly independent sources that together increases reliability. Partly - because Tomas, who reckons himself as a skeptic, had of course seen the French pictures, but still without having anything to gain from any image manipulation - rather the contrary!

- Hege has made an appointment with the people behind "Visit Hessdalen" at seven o'clock. On their facebook pages, she has seen some nice block candles for sale, and asked where to buy them? No problem, - they can open the store just for us, even if it's Sunday and outside opening hours. Visit Hessdalen, Hilde Vårhus, together with her husband, Bjørn Vik, runs a UFO camp and a UFO kiosk in Hessdalen, - yes, they even run a UFO pub that is open at irregular intervals. The kiosk holds all kinds of souvenirs, with and without a UFO motif.

There has been some tourism in Hessdalen, but far from enough to make it possible to live on it, for the time being. Hilde and Bjørn also run Visit Hessdalen alongside regular jobs. In a way, I still have an ambivalent relationship with this mix of UFOs, Hessdalen and tourism; It is good if someone is able to take advantage of the potential that undoubtedly is there, but at the same time I'm afraid that skeptics and debunkers will suggest that there are commercial interests in the picture. Currently, and in the foreseeable future, there's no reason to suggest anything like that. This is run on a very small scale. And Hilde and Bjørn in Visit Hessdalen are nice people, and I just want to wish them luck!

Having said goodbye to Hilde and Bjørn, we drive directly into Båttjønndalen and park at "our" cliff - the highest point at the road. It's been raining more and more over the afternoon and evening, and now we don't see a single star. Dense cloud cover. After one and a half hours we freeze so much in the gusts of wind, that we feel like moving and at the same time getting warmed up a little in the car.

At the bottom of Finnsådalen, just before the road turns off towards Vårhuskjølen, we see a light in the direction of the northeast. To the left of Mount Rogne. Is it a planet? No, there is still dense cloud cover, - and besides, it's moving. Across the valley, from east to west. Is it an airplane? The light goes exceptionally low, and there is no flashing lights on it. Only a steady yellow light. We stop and leave the car, bring out the camera and start recording. The light seems to pass over Aspåskjølen and is heading for Mount Finnsåhøgda. After half a minute, it has disappeared behind the mountain, well below the top. The northern end of Finnsåhøgda is less than 1000 meters high. The light could not have flown in more than 800-900 meters altitude. I check the flight radar app on my phone that shows that there are currently no aircrafts nearby. We have a certain feeling that this is one of those "sailplanes" that we saw in Easter, and last in July. But, unlike before, it's a cloudy evening. Maybe it doesn't matter so much if it's starlit or cloudy anyway?

Monday we check both the alarm camera in the Blue Box and the log of Science Camp. No "sailplanes" any of the places. It'll be wrong angle in relation to the alarm camera, so I hadn't expected that either, but we had good hope that at least the base up on Finnsåhøgda would register this, film and photograph. Their log, however, only shows camera trouble, weather data, and a couple of cars and headlamp mis-observations. The headlamps could by the way have been us on our way back to the car...

At home, I transfer our film from camera to PC. The phenomenon is captured, but again it only shows a small, luminous dot against an otherwise dark background without reference. It doesn't make us any wiser…

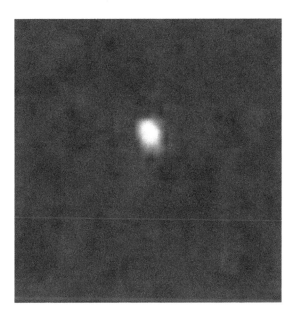

It doesn't make us any wiser…

16 SOLUTION IN SIX YEARS? SCEPTICAL!

Friday, October 19th. Science Camp is over, but there's still lights at the community center when we pass we pass 9.30 pm. The students have already traveled home, but the management is supposed to stay in Hessdalen until tomorrow morning. Possibly they're sitting and debriefing the last fourteen days of work?

At NRK.no is an interview with Anna-Lena Tjøniksen, operational manager for the data park inside the new research station at Skarvan. She's a professor of chemistry at Østfold University. She thinks it might take up to several years to get an answer to what the Hessdalen phenomenon is - even if the observation base is manned 24/7. Hauge is also interviewed in the same article. He says; - By starting 24-hour continuous measurements over a three-year period - then we should start to have statistics that show everything that stands out from the normal. I believe that in about six years, we should be close to a solution.

Well... we disagree... In our opinion research is being done in wrong direction and agree with Jon Arvid: They are astray!

Several observations have been made during this year's field action.

Including Thursday night last week, according to the NRK article:

> *- A bright light moved horizontally with zigzag movements. The light was seen towards the northwestern part of the valley, with a mountain side as background. The research group says they characterize the observation as interesting.*

We don't believe the research group ever will be able to find out anything relevant at all, - by using instruments that measure field strength and seismic activity, respectively - which are examples mentioned in the article...

But the question is whether a 24-hour research station will affect the phenomenon in any way; will there be less of it? Fewer observations? Will the UFOs simply disappear from Hessdalen? We discuss this when we park at Slettælet. It's dark up on Skarvan right now at least. No one at work...

On the other hand; In fact, if there's an intelligence behind the phenomena in Hessdalen – a technology far exceeding human technology of today - is it perhaps easy for this hypothetical intelligence to thwart Hauge & co? Bypass the cameras and put measuring instruments out of play, etc.?

During the very first field action under the auspices of Project Hessdalen in 1984, one experienced "accidents" with the measuring instruments, - to the extent that Erling Strand mentioned it in the final report:

> *"Several times during the project period, the cameras did not work. This happened mainly when we needed them the most. Such events should also have been recorded. Also other instruments stopped working when we needed them most, mainly due to too little voltage, or too poor power connection. All such things should be noted."*

Also Havik wrote something about this; they experienced that the power turned off in the caravan with instruments, - a phenomenon passed, - and the power returned. I also recall to have read that Blue Box often has been out of service in connection with observations.

Moreover, people living in Hessdalen have reported phenomena beyond reach of the alarm camera - which only covers a certain radius and angle of Hessdalen. Phenomena are apparently often observed over the Blue Box, behind and beside it etc.

The following observation by Bjørn and Bjarne Lillevold from 2002 is illustrative:

> *"Bjørn and Bjarne was working on a car out in the driveyard, at home in Vårhus. Then they saw a large, black "rod", which stood vertically, just behind Blue Box. The lower part of the "rod" flashed occasionally. It was a blue-green light. There could be several minutes between each blink. The "rod" moved slowly southwards towards Rognsåsjøen. After 15 minutes it came behind the mountain."(Source: hessdalen.org).*

Another thing is what the alarm camera actually detects from what is happening *within* radius. Friday two weeks ago, it was like New Year's Eve, but the alarm camera didn't register anything of the activity.

At Slettælet, little or nothing happens. There is dense cloud cover, and neither stars nor planets are to be seen. This weekend it's almost full moon, but the moon is behind the clouds as well. We don't care; - last weekend we experienced a phenomenon under the cloud cover, so there is no reason to lose faith.

An hour later we drive into Båttjønndalen instead, zero and nothing, - then we take the usual trip up on Aspåskjølen. Nada. Around midnight it starts to rain, and we decide to call it a night. According to the weather forecast, there will be sun and blue skies in the middle of the day tomorrow. It promises good, since I am ready to photograph a little during daytime this weekend.

After we came home the last time a new picture appeared from the French Pierre Beake. Again it was taken during broad daylight, and again the phenomenon was seen when zooming in on the PC afterwards. The picture shows a seemingly metallic, ball-like object, with some kind of lights. The picture is taken inside west Lake Øyongen, in the direction of mount Morkavollhøgda.

Hege received a message from Tomas Dahl after the picture was published; it's very similar to his daylight photo taken in 2016, which Tomas also points out. Not only do the two photos look similar, - they are also taken in about the same place and in the same direction - towards the south-southeast and Morkavollhøgda!

The picture, as well as an article titled "Is this the Hessdalen phenomenon?", was published on the NEA radio's facebook page. Here was some discussion in the comment field about whether the image was authentic or not. One person maintained that the "phenomenon" had "been helped" to end up on the picture, and that the picture was tampered with. This was justified by the fact that if one zoomed in, one could see a "blurred" square around the object - as if it were "copy-pasted" in photoshop.

I had also noticed this myself when zooming in, but a google search informs that this is a common effect with pictures stored in JPEG format (as Beakes image was stored in). The image deteriorates with repeated storage, - a phenomenon called JPEG artifact. The "blurred" square is thus not at all a striking argument against Pierre Beake and his Col de vence team.

However, I do a little more googling around Beake and find that he has a DVD movie and a book for sale through his website. He has also photographed a UFO in broad daylight before, in England, in connection with crop circles. Hm ... The more I read about the guy, the more skeptical I become. Had it not been for Tomas' image, which in a way also confirms Beake's image, I would have been super-skeptical!

On the other hand; If Beake really fakes his UFO photos, he wouldn't have to travel all the way to Hessdalen to do that - he could very well have used photoshop at home in France instead? Also, if he caught the first pictures in 2015 - including a flying saucer in Hessdalen - then he should have topped those pictures with something even more spectacular now - a saucer with windows and landing gear or something - if the idea is to make money ? Instead, it is a kind of opposite development. The picture taken now October 5 is clearly less spectacular than the 2015 pictures. It shows something that looks like a technical object - yes, but not some of the "classic" UFO shapes, - saucer / cigar / triangle etc. Instead, it looks like a thing with lights on and some strange protruding hose pipe-like All in all it seems almost homemade, - with gaffa tape etc. The "craft" doesn't look very aerodynamic!

It must also be mentioned that, in addition to the pictures from Pierre Beake and Tomas Dahl, there is a third daylight photo; - Kåre Gøran Tjelte took several landscape photos from Vårhus in the direction of southwest 14th August 2015 at. 5.46 - the same day Beake got his alleged saucer image - and one of these shows a metallic-looking object, - a kind of square object.

This alone is not sufficient for documentation, but in context, three independent sources strengthen the reliability. A bit on the way, these pictures can thus be taken to confirm Hessdalen residents stories of crafts seen in broad daylight, - daylight discs!

- Three pictures and three photographers! Hopefully I will be the fourth, I think while we drive inwards towards Lake Øyongen Saturday morning. We drive the toll road to the end and park at the foot of Mount Kåshøgda. From here we look inwards towards Lake Elgsjøen in the south, and towards Valley Båttjønndalen in the north. In front of us we have the huge, wide Lake Øyongen. The weather is impeccable; sun from blue sky. I take pictures right and left. Great scenery, at least...

After having dinner, we drive to Slettælet. It's not more than 6:30 pm, but it's almost dark already. At Slettælet there is a motorhome parked we notice. More people out in the same errands tonight... It has become cloudy during the afternoon and there are no visible stars in the sky.

Later, we need to go back to the cabin and pick up some clothes. On the way back up to the main road, we see a large, bright light over Hessdalskjølen i the northeast. The light is moving! Sloping towards us! I brake, jump out of the car and press record on the camera. All this in a matter of seconds. Still, I'm too late. The light has dimmed down, and again it's just dark over Hessdalskølen. Soon afterwards, there's a white flash, but now slightly to the left of where the light dimmed. Is it a plane? I check the flight operator, and quite right: Here comes the flight Trondheim - Oslo...

Was it just a plane all the time?

The first light we saw, was that the plane? No - the light we saw first was big and yellow! A large, luminous, yellow sphere. The only times I've experienced airplanes that way are with the landing lights turned on just before landing. *Then* airplanes can remind of what we just saw. But the plane that passes in Hessdalen now took OFF from Værnes airport a few minutes ago! Therefore, there must have been two separate lights; the flight on it's way to Oslo, AND another light that disappeared when it met the plane...

Have we just seen what Jon Arvid has been talking about several times, - and besides Leif Havik has mentioned? That "it dims when airplanes pass"? Under the section "The UFO phenomenon often has an intelligent behavior" Havik writes:

"How could it happen that several people in Hessdalen over the past 5 years, have seen that the light phenomenon dimmed the lights when it encountered airplanes? I myself have seen this, even though it was just once. On September 9, 1982, a family
of three, as well as a fire guard, saw a light phenomenon at Toppenish Ridge in Yakima. The time was 10.25 pm, and when a liner arrived, the light phenomenon
dimmed the lights so that it could only be glimpsed. About a minute later, the original
light came back."

We drive up to Aspåskjølen and park. Too bad we didn't arrive here ten minutes ago, - then we would have had ringside seats. But again, it's no easy matter to get close to the phenomenon... If we are one place, then it passes another...

--

- Back at the cabin, Hege asks the million dollar question: "What we have seen, - What do you think it is?"

- As in, what are UFOs? Wow! When I think about it, I'm actually not sure what I think. Honestly. - At least I am sure that the UFO phenomenon in Hessdalen and the UFO phenomenon globally represents one and the same phenomenon, understood that phenomena in Hessdalen are the UFO phenomenon globally - in miniature. In other words, a solution to what's happening in Hessdalen implies a solution to the UFO phenomenon as a whole, - globally and totally.

We have primarily seen lights in category 1 (flash) and category 2 (yellow and white lights that move around in the valley). Only on one occasion have we seen category 3 – several lights together, which appeared as if they were attached to an object. However, I feel that I have a basis for claiming that geophysical theories related to plasma *alone* are inadequate.

Because; - can a gas move over a mile, in a steady path and steady speed through Hessdalen, - completely unaffected by the weather and wind? Can two bright spots of gas move completely synchronously, and dim down the lights completely synchronously? Hardly...

Hauge & co's. hypotheses of a hitherto undiscovered natural phenomenon, related to the geophysical and atmospheric conditions in Hessdalen, are insufficient, in my opinion. Not as the *only* explanation!

But: It may be, - as Erling Strand is talking about - that two (or more) phenomena exist in parallel in Hessdalen. Teodorani has also raised the question of whether (at least) two widely different phenomena coexist in Hessdalen, or whether it's the same phenomenon that occurs in different physical conditions.

During the EMBLA field actions in the early 2000s, Teodorani himself experienced structured, solid objects in Hessdalen, which eventually led him to the inclusion of the ET hypothesis in his considerations regarding Hessdalen.

At the same time, Teodorani suggested secret military experiments with exotic technology as an alternative possibility.

Although I feel that the military hypothesis is becoming less and less relevant the more I see of this. The way the phenomenon appear like "jack in the box" and disappears into nothing, does not give associations to military activity, is my gut feeling.

Another thing is - if you look beyond Hessdalen, - that the UFO phenomenon has been relatively consistent over time - ever since the term "flying saucers" appeared in 1947. If the UFOs represent an ongoing military project where one is experimenting with exotic technology, wouldn't one expect a kind of UFO "evolution" with ever-improved design and performance? It has been 37 years since it broke loose in Hessdalen, but it's largely the same things that is reported nowadays, as in the 80s... - no progression and development?

So, if the plasma/natural phenomena hypotheses are insufficient and the military hypothesis can be written off in the long run (?), one is left with some form of "visitation"? Perhaps ET have a base deep in the mountains in and around Hessdalen, as suggested in the novel by Thomassen? Or can Hessdalen represent a kind of charging station where "visitors" drop by to fill "petrol"? Or is Hessdalen a kind of "portal" for "long-distance travelers", with "arrivals and departure"?

Or is the explanation perhaps even more exotic? Is it perhaps a glimpse into another world, another dimension? "Where did they come from, and where did they go", said Leif Havik in connection with some of his observations in Hessdalen...

I've seen phenomena appear out of nowhere, be visible in minutes, then just disappear as suddenly as they appeared myself. Could it be that Hessdalen is a kind of "window" where the boundaries are "indistinct"? Where it's possible to look into another reality, parallel to our own? Do we need to revolutionize our understanding of the physical world in order to understand the phenomena in Hessdalen -

in order to understand the UFO phenomenon?

--

- We're in November, and it's now one year since our first "observation trip" to Hessdalen. Since then we've stayed in the valley regularly - mostly every other weekend, as well as most of the holidays. We've huddled through ice-cold winter evenings at Aspåskjølen, sweating us up on Mount Finnsåhøgda in thirty plus mid-summer, stayed a week in Båttjøndalen Valley in a tent without getting fish, been eaten by mosquitoes and hunted by wasps, climbed ten mountains higher than thousand meters in and around Hessdalen, driven a distance corresponding to Trondheim - Oslo - back and forth - along bumpy gravel roads with sheep that will not move - and not the least - observed for hundreds of hours in clear weather, rain, sleet, snow, hail, gale and storm.

We've talked to young and old residents of Hessdalen, people who have seen a lot and people who have seen little…

- -

Are you going to be here for two days? said Jon Arvid … - If you had been here for two *years* you might have had the chance to see what I've seen…
This is just the *first* year…

CPSIA information can be obtained
at www.ICGtesting.com
Printed in the USA
LVHW080631200422
716646LV00007B/368